I0438836

# Average
# American
# Politics

by

## Cory Merry

Strategic Book Group

Copyright © 2010

All rights reserved – Cory Merry

No part of this book may be reproduced or transmitted
in any form or by any means, graphic, electronic, or
mechanical, including photocopying, recording, taping,
or by any information storage retrieval system, without
the permission, in writing, from the publisher.

Strategic Book Group
P.O. Box 333
Durham CT 06422
www.StrategicBookClub.com

ISBN: 978-1-60976-091-5

Printed in the United States of America

Book Design: Bonita S. Watson

# *Dedication*

This book is dedicated to my beautiful wife, Lucky, my two incredible daughters, Marissa and Tiffany, and my mother and father, JoAnn and Loyd. Without their support, rearing, and unconditional love, I could never have finished this book.

It is also dedicated to my friends at BBB Systems who gave me the first platform on which to write on a regular basis and my first experience on radio. Had I not stumbled onto their website, www.voiceofarizona.com, all those many years ago while searching for a place to voice my opinions I would never have realized I was interested in such a diverse subject matter. I would like to offer a special thanks to Robin O'dell of The Proofreading Boutique in Tampa Florida. Her editing of this book was incredible.

This book is also dedicated to those men and women serving and who have served in the Armed Forces of the United States. Because you can't, I will. Thank you for your service.

# Contents

# *Introduction*

When I sat down to start this book it was based on what I thought about a variety of subjects. But in the course of writing it I have changed it around a half dozen times at least. The final version is as much an education for the common man and woman in America as it is a guide to move you through some of the harder topics to understand. I tried to follow the KISS philosophy: Keep It Simple Stupid. And I think I accomplished this to a greater degree than I thought possible. But on some subjects in American politics, simple isn't an option because the topics themselves are not simple. Where simplicity could be applied I did so, but where the fundamental questions and answers were harder to come by, I went more in depth into the subject.

I believe that America is the greatest country on earth for two reasons and two reasons only:
1. The Intricate Simplicity of the US Constitution
2. The American People

As you read this book I wish that you come away with only one thing, an understanding of how important our freedom to debate truly is. Whether it be in the halls of Congress, the Oval

Office, the Supreme Court, or the corner deli, we have retained for ourselves one of the most important rights anywhere on this planet, and that is to not only have an opinion, but to share it with others while trying to move them to believe the same way.

Freedom of speech is not only a fundamental right, it is the best tool we Americans have with which to move our country both forward and backward. Oftentimes I have been in debates (conversations for the newly anointed) and heard people say what should be happening. I usually ask them why they don't run for office if they have all the answers. The answer is almost always the same. They wouldn't know what to do once they got there and got all the information.

That makes sense until I ask them what part of the equation they think they are missing. The reply is always the same: the facts. Well facts are stubborn things and even with all the facts you can still make a bad decision unless you are guided by core principles. One thing we in America are not really good at is getting to the bottom of the problem. We are great at addressing the issues at hand and we usually do this in one of two ways: throw money at it or make it a part of government, which in turn throws money at it.

But America was not born out of the idea that government is the answer to what ails us, it was founded on the idea that people are capable of doing most things for themselves if only government stays out of their way long enough to solve the problem.

This is not to suggest that there is no role for government in the broader sense of the American experience. Of course we need a government. In America government was created by the people, not by some ruling-class elite. And in the Constitution this government's job was uniquely defined. It was to serve the people in those things the people could not otherwise provide for themselves. The government's job is simplistic: national defense, international trade, oversight of trade between the states themselves, and other jobs so large that, individually, Americans could never handle them personally. It was all based on the sovereignty of the people as equal to the monarchies of Europe.

They created government so that there was a place to vest those responsibilities for the mutual benefit of all Americans.

While sovereignty is not a new concept, American sovereignty is unique. Not just national sovereignty but individual sovereignty. Americans had the audacity, at least in the king's eyes, of believing themselves above and below no other man on earth. We felt confident that unlike those countries that had a leader, we could all be leaders and owners of our own destinies and not simply born into our lot in life where we would stay for the duration.

These are a few of the ideas explained in this book along with specific areas where America has made monumental mistakes based purely on a disregard of our original core beliefs. You and I are the kings and queens of this country and as such we are subservient to no power other than the power we elect to charge others with to exercise on our behalf and for our benefit. Government is a tool created in this case of the people, for the people, and administered by the people. We choose who will use the power we give and we decide how much power we give them. If they are doing things we don't want them to be doing with the power we temporarily grant them, it then becomes our responsibility to remove them from those positions and access to that very power.

I cover a few things that are everyday news and a few that are not, but are just as important even though they do not garner the coverage like the others. Among them is government's ever-increasing role in our lives as provider and how this affects your very paycheck; federal government's usurpation of state and local government rights and responsibilities and how it affects your everyday life; bad federal law and how it affected the debate on abortion in this country and the precedent it has created for future acts by the Supreme Court; the US Tax Code and why it matters to you what everyone else pays; protecting our military men and women and our elderly and understanding why they are at risk; and the ever-popular situation regarding immigration in this country and how it really does affect your world. Toward the end of the book you will find some short essays I wrote over the years while working on the book that cover a few more topics that you might find interesting. Each one could be a book in itself.

While it is easy to sit back and complain about what is wrong with America I go a step further than most people do and remind you of what you can do to change things for the better. You will not find another person more devoted to the notions that America is still the greatest country on earth and that that greatness stems from her people. Since the beginning of this great experiment in self-rule, the power to shape and reshape the nation has been in your hands, quite literally. Every height of modern marvel we have achieved and every low we have experienced has been because of the American people and how they exercised this power. Either because of their constant vigilance or rooted in their lack thereof, America has ebbed and flowed based on her people.

We have corrected many wrongs that were built into our founding, from slavery to a woman's right to vote to the way we treat the least among us, we have learned from our mistakes and made the necessary corrections to live up to the promise of our founding, that being the concept that all men are created equal, every person counts, and every person matters regardless of race, creed, or ability.

Before you go any further I want you to take a moment and think about what that means, the Promise of America. From the words on the Statue of Liberty to the wording of the Declaration of Independence and the US Constitution, we were determined to be a great people right from the start. So no matter how upset you get as you read this book, keep in mind that when it is over, the solution is also revealed and though the solution is not earth-shattering—in fact, you already know what it is—it is truly in your hands to change any of the ills we face, just as it was designed to be and just as it has always been.

Good reading …

# *Chapter 1*

The government of the United States of America is ill suited for its current role as father figure and provider for the masses.

Many times over the last fifty years the government has set out with the purest of intentions to eradicate a problem only to deepen or worsen the problem. Cases in point: Social Security and Welfare.

Social Security was created during the Great Depression from an amalgamation of different state-run programs to help the poor and the infirm elderly population. It was never designed for the number of people who currently receive benefits from the program. It was never designed to allow for survivor benefits to underage children of deceased parents nor for drug addicts who cannot work due to their "illness." Although modified several times over the decades to accommodate or create these recipients, it cannot be sustained in its current or any other form. There simply are not enough people paying in for the growing number of recipients. At some point in the very near future the system will simply have to be scrapped or the tax rate for Social Security will have to become so large that it bankrupts the nation as a whole.

Welfare was created out of this same desire and obligation we have as a united people to assist those most in need. The system has been bastardized over the decades since LBJ first championed his idea of the Great Society, allowing for families benefiting from the system to raise their incomes by simply increasing the number of mouths they have to feed. It has also shifted focus away from the entire family unit and begun to concentrate on the single-parent family, which most of the time reflects a mother and children. In these cases, early on in the program's life, it began to de-emphasize the importance of the two-parent home, thus leading to a change in the way society as a whole viewed the situation. Fathers, it was determined in many minority communities, were not important and began to be phased out of the equation all together as mothers discovered that the state would step in and fill the role of father and provider. This was not a conscious decision but one of the many unintended consequences of the program. This in and of itself has led to an increase in poverty and minority children having a less advantageous start in life.

This all sounds like opinion but now let us look deeper into the situations mentioned earlier. To begin with we should look at that opening statement in its broadest sense: The government of the United States of America is ill suited for its current role as father figure and provider for the masses. Liberals from Seattle to New York will tell you part of the government's job is to "provide for those people who cannot provide for themselves." Conservatives from Los Angeles to Washington will tell you that it is the people of this country who are best suited to solve the problems within the country when it comes to poverty, homelessness, and unemployment. While both have validity and most Americans agree with both sides of the argument, where the real debate comes into play is to what degree this "providing" should happen.

If we look at any number of programs that have been implemented by our government over the last one hundred years, we will see that the good intentions of the past have contributed little to end or even lessen the problems they were intended to solve.

Social Security, the so-called Fourth Leg of politics and quite literally the Holy Grail of the Democratic Party and perhaps the most steep of mountains to be climbed, is by far the most well known and probably stands as the best example of a government program that has grown out of control. Social Security has been changed so heinously from its original concept that I really doubt whether Franklin Roosevelt would even recognize it today. For millions of retirees it has been a saving grace, allowing them to live if not a glamorous life, one that at least ensures they eat in retirement. But in the same breath that accomplished this minor feat, the program also created a mentality that the government owes the elderly something that constitutionally it does not: the freedom to retire without want, having all their needs met. While we all know that the program was never intended to be the sole supporting financial factor in retirees' lives, many older Americans resent the program today because it gave them false hope about what part or how small a part they would have to play in preparing for their own retirement. Many believe that had they really thought about the cost of retirement, the longer life span of Americans today, and the constantly rising cost of living, *not* having Social Security dangling out there might have driven them to prepare more for the future on their own and probably would have resulted in an even higher standard of living during their retirement years.

Here's a theory for you that just might expand your thought process. If we had not had Social Security over the last seventy-five years, do you think there would be a higher savings rate in this country or a lower one? Second question: Had we not had Social Security, do you think we would have experienced the incredible economic growth as a nation, considering the very low savings rate we experienced during the same time? And, finally, would we be in the current financial situation we are in as a nation had we had a higher savings rate and lower investment dollars circulating through the system (which might have provided for more cash buying power for the individual and made financing smaller-ticket items like clothing, furniture, and appliances unnecessary)? In other words, could it be that because of the false sense of security created by the Social Security program people spent more than they should have, creating the opportunity for more people to be in these bad home loans and forcing some corporations to become creative with their books to meet the expected growth that this kind of investment should produce? I'm not a professor of economics, but I believe a thesis based on that idea would get some starving college student either an A for effort or thrown out of the liberal institution of their choice.

Back to the topic at hand. The trickle-down education part of this situation is even worse. The generation who followed those who were first covered by Social Security in the 1930s has grown up with this idea embedded in their minds since birth: "The government is going to be there to help you in retirement." Between that mentality and the poor example set by many of their parents, in the very near future the situation is not going to get better but worse for this generation. There is another side to this. Many younger Americans are beginning to resent the money taken from their paychecks each week and given to not just the elderly, but to the multiple other people who now qualify for the benefits regardless of age. As I mentioned earlier, the system has been so heinously altered over the years to allow other groups of people to draw upon it that Roosevelt wouldn't recognize it, although he might applaud it, as you will see later. Even beyond that, many more in the younger generations have access to more information and news because the major media's grip on controlling the subject matter is being weakened by the new media of the Internet, talk radio, and cable TV. While two of the three aren't really all that new, their use has changed dramatically over the last twenty years.

At this point we need to have a real discussion about the Social Security system and the very real problems it faces. But more important, we need to focus on steps that can be taken to secure the future for ourselves, our children, and even our parents' generation.

Before any real solutions can be hashed out, we need to make sure we are dealing with the facts of the situation. The news reports seem to make it pretty clear that even those who run the program and its healthcare partner, Medicare, know what's coming:

> Medicare is paying out more than it receives, and Social Security will start paying out more in benefits than it collects in taxes in 2016, one year sooner than projected last year, trustees for the two main safety nets for retirees said Tuesday. Social Security, the giant trust fund, will be depleted by 2037, four years sooner than projected. Medicare will be insolvent by 2017, two years earlier than the date last projected, the trustees said. The recession is cutting payroll-tax contributions just as the baby-boom generation begins to *retire*. (*Chicago Sun Times*, May 13, 2009)

The scariest part of that story is this line: "two years earlier than projected last year …"

So this isn't a news flash for the people in charge. It seems they have been running the clock down on Social Security for decades, knowing that it could not sustain itself long term. I remember my Aunt Martha was upset back in the 1980s because President Reagan had extended the retirement age from sixty-five to sixty-seven. She was sixty-four when that happened. It was the year of her birth affected by the change. I was thirteen or fourteen and I remember that's when I first found out that there were issues with the system. Of course, I didn't care back then. I was still a kid. But when my interest peaked some years later I asked her surviving husband about it to make sure I understood what happened as it applied to them. It is a continuing theme throughout government's history; sacrifices have to be made by the few sometimes for the benefit of the larger majority. It makes sense, but we have been dealing with the problem since way before that.

I did a Google search on "History of Social Security Insolvency" and found multiple sites that go far deeper into the situation then I am going to go in this book. The most nonemotional site I found was this one: http://www.nysscpa.org/cpajournal/2006/506/infocus/p20.htm. CPA's have a way of making sense out of this puzzle far better than I do. I would encourage you to do a little research for yourself here and at the other sites that come up.

If you do go to this site you will see that in the 1950s the system was expanded to cover the disabled, one of the many expansions in benefits that has happened over the decades. You will also see that in the early 1980s, Congress, those magical people we sent to Washington, made an error that nearly killed the system financially within a few years.

The solutions to the problems are no easier than the problems themselves.

So with the problems so large, what are the answers? Well, here are a few to get us started. Liberals will tell you that all we have to do is increase the cap on who pays Social Security taxes. In our current system every person who works pays SSI taxes on every penny they make up to $106,000, and then not one more penny no matter how much you make. So what is wrong with this idea? Plenty.

One of the benefits of making over $106,000 a year as a single person, or $212,000 as a couple, is you now have the honor of paying an exorbitant amount in income taxes. These are the taxes that fund everything else the government spends money on. These taxes go into the general fund. And one dirty little secret is that nearly 50 percent of all income taxes come from these people even though they represent less than 10 percent of the total population. Another dirty little secret about SSI is that the money is supposedly locked away in special accounts managed by Uncle Sam. The only problem with this idea is that it is not true, at all. Social Security also goes into the general fund and has for decades. Regardless of who has been in the White House or in control of Congress, the money keeps "leaking" or, more accurately, being diverted into the general fund. This money has been used for everything from roadwork to military spending to financing the arts and abortion. If there is a government vehicle for distribution, some of your money that is for your "retirement" has made its way into it.

The ideas that your money is sitting someplace safe or that your beloved parents are spending it with the understanding that your children will pay your way in the future are asinine. Can you afford to support two other people right now? Nobody can, at least not anyone making less than that top tax bracket, and, to be honest, many of them can't either. Funny thing about Americans, we tend to spend what we make and just a hair more, no matter what we make. No, folks, that money is el gonzo. It was never really there. Even former president Bill Clinton's so-called surplus of $1,000,000,000,000.00 (that's one trillion dollars for those of you who are unsure) was really just Social Security if we didn't tap into it for ten years. A pipe dream if ever there was one in Washington; as if that was ever really going to happen. Even former president George W. Bush (I say *even* because most liberals and some conservatives thought the man was stupid) understood that the money was not there. Remember that story about him wanting to see the IOUs in the box? Maybe he wasn't a rocket scientist, but he got the concept of "there isn't any money in the box."

Some liberals will be honest and tell you that some of the SSI money is sitting in treasury notes and bonds. While this may be true, it is supposed to be given to the retirees and others who have qualified for the money. And again, those are nothing more than debts paid by the government with interest.

Conservatives approach Social Security from an entirely different angle. They believe that Social Security was, from the start, designed to do two things and two things only: grow dependency on government and provide a built-in voter block for the Democratic Party. Whether this was FDR's plan all along or not may be debatable, but it is a very real side effect of the system nonetheless. Elderly people, and anyone gaining

ground on being elderly, have come to shudder anytime a
suggestion is made about reforming, changing, or in some other
way attempting to make the system work better or even trying
to make it solvent by any means other than raising taxes. They
tend to vote Democratic in elections based on fear tactics that
the Left uses to motivate them. "Republicans are going to take
away your Social Security checks" and "That money is yours,
you worked hard for it, don't let them take it away from you,"
followed by the all-too-popular "Do you want your grandmother
eating dog food?" Which seems to be effective come election
time and usually turns out some voters to the polls.

Early in his administration, President George W. Bush tried
and failed to get legislation passed that would have given the
people control over a portion of their Social Security accounts.
That's right, their accounts. Every American from grade school
up needs to be taught this very important lesson: The government
of the United States of America has no money. It does not produce
a single commodity that adds to the economy of the country.
The only money Uncle Sam has to work with is your money. It
takes money from you in a number of ways, the most common
being taxes, fines, and fees. So anytime you hear some politician
say they want to invest in education, roads, space exploration,
or anything else, ask yourself one basic question: What is this
going to cost me?

The very idea of giving people control over their own
retirement accounts through Social Security should not be a
point of contention with either party. Yet it is, with both.

Liberals don't like the idea because they claim you are not
an expert in money management. This from the same people
who have run massive deficits in this country for decades.
Democrats also say that the system will not support the elderly if
the young remove their money from the plan. Well, let's see, we
didn't have the money to fight in Iraq or Afghanistan, we didn't
have the money to bail out the banks, insurance companies,
automakers, or the states of California and Maine, but somehow
we figured out a way to do all of these things and pay the elderly

their Social Security. Oh, that's right, we just borrowed it. Not a good plan, yet it has kept us afloat. However, it will not keep working forever. Just ask GM.

Meanwhile, the Right will tell you that the stock market has averaged a 10 percent return per year during any decade you want to look at, even those that include 1929 or 1987, the two biggest drops until recently. And even now, in the aftermath of the devastating fall of the Dow Jones Industrial Average, we have seen in excess of a 25 percent jump since its low on March 19, 2009.

So what about this idea of the stock market and the money going in there being under our control, individually? If George W. Bush would have gotten his way it would not have stopped the problems immediately and many might be worse off today because of it, but he was only talking about 2 percent of our SSI taxes being under our direct control, not all of it. What if they did give you control over all of it? How might that work?

Let's say that you had control over just the money you would earn for the rest of your working life from here on out. The government takes 15.3 percent of your income for Social Security and Medicare right now. According to the site mentioned earlier in this chapter, that is the amount we are talking about. Let's say you and your spouse combined make $45,000 per year. They take 7.65 percent from you, as they do now, and 7.65 percent from your employer. Right away you are getting a 100 percent return on your investment. How, you ask? Because you are only paying half of the 15.3 percent and your employer is paying the other half (which could have been a raise for you but, tough crap, this is America and we have to play by these stupid rules). We will start with one year's earning into the system and work our way up from there, just to keep it simple.

You make $45,000 in household income per year of which 15.3 percent is invested into the market in any number of ways but which averages 10 percent per year return. So, 15.3 percent of $45,000 is $6,885 in the first year with not a dime of interest on it, which of course you would start gaining immediately, but that is beyond my limited understanding of the situation. So,

$6,885 and another $6,885 per year every year until you are age sixty-five. We will say you are forty so we have twenty-five years of this to do. It would equal over $750,000 with a 10 percent return per year on average. Some years will be better and some worse. Keep in mind this is if you never get a raise in your income, either one of you, for twenty-five years. But work just two years longer and you would have over $920,000. This comes from the amazing power of compound interest. Imagine if people started at twenty-one making just $25,000 per year and never got a raise. That's $3,835 per year with forty-four years and not a raise until retirement.... It's a whopping $2,757,000.05. I want my kids to have that money for themselves, sorry, folks. Call me stingy but they will work just as hard as I do, if not harder considering the taxes they will have to pay in the future. I don't know about you, but that just opened my eyes big-time. I actually just called both of my nineteen-year-old daughters and told them to get ready to be rich.

Let's pretend that your parents make about $1,300 and $1,600 from their Social Security checks each month. Let's say they lived to be the average of eighty-six years and had retired at sixty-five with just that money to survive on, pretending they don't have a dime in savings. They will go through $780,000 dollars before they pass on. Now if they have their bills in line, which we will say they do, they can live pretty well on that money. But if they had started saving as we just discovered together, they would never have needed Social Security.

What returns this kind of money each year? The big boys on the stock exchange, the Blue Chips. GM, Ford (I know what you are thinking, but they will come back and it's a buyers market right now for their stock), GE, IBM, AT&T, Coke, and a list of others. This isn't opinion at this point, people. These are the facts right out of the history books and a site I found: http://www.moneychimp.com/calculator/compound_interest_calculator.htm. Use it to discover your potential income in retirement as soon as you put this book down. In fact, go to it now. I'll wait....

Did you go? You did—I see it all over your face. Some of you are wishing you'd known about this sooner; others are thinking,

"Hot damn, I'm going to be rich"; and others are thinking, "I can still put some away for the future but my kids are going to be filthy rich if they just keep at it." Now you know why I called my kids moments ago.

So if you look at what George W. Bush wanted to start, it doesn't seem so scary now. If you are smart you will learn to live on 84.7 percent of your income now and do this anyway. If you are in debt, get out of it. Dave Ramsey has a working plan that hundreds of thousands have gotten into and paid off their debt quickly without shelling out money to someone else. You can find more on Dave Ramsey here: www.daveramsey.com.

It is really the simplest way to become debt free, and once you accomplish that, you are set to explode your investing opportunities. Even if you are Mr. Play-it-Safe and just want to put massive amounts of cash into savings accounts, just remember you are losing money there, too, because inflation goes up faster than interest rates. But that is really Dave Ramsey's specialty; listen to him on that, not me.

So why doesn't Uncle Sam want us to depend on ourselves? It's a strange question for a country like America to even have to ask. The simple answer is votes. Dependency breeds dependents. Politicians want to get reelected and they think you are stupid. Plain and simple, those are the reasons. Hurts, don't it?

What really chafes them is that many of you have at your disposal a way to invest like this using only a portion of the money we were just talking about. The 401(k) is just such a mechanism, as is the IRA. With the IRA you still foot the entire bill for the investments, but with the 401(k) you don't always have to. Many of you have, through your employers, what are called Matching 401(k)s. That is where you put in a percentage and the employer matches the contribution with one of their own into your account. It is sort of like the Social Security plan, but you control it all. And when you leave, you take it with you and roll it into another 401(k) at your new employer or it moves directly into the IRA of your choice, giving you another vehicle to grow your wealth.

So why don't we do this anyway? Well, because we tend to be selfish creatures. It's true, like it or not. None of us is living twenty-five years in the future. We are living today. And, damn it, we want to live and not have those old versions of ourselves sitting around complaining that they didn't *do* anything. Well, if you really want to make those old people happy, take care of them today. Just a little, as I have shown you, will go a long way to making those people happy one day.

But perhaps there is a place for the US Government in all this after all. Look, right now we have a ton of options in which to invest our money, but most of us do not. If there is one thing we know about the government it is that they can force us to do a lot of things that are not for our own good, so why not take a lick at doing something that is for our own good and our government's good as well? Free us from the system of dependency on them.

Here's how my plan might work. I say *might* because I am no economist, I'm not a mathematician, and I sure as hell am not a lawyer, so the legalese of what I am proposing will surely have to be worked out at some point if it ever sees the light of day.

## The Average American Personal Retirement Plan

The government sets up a plan within a plan. We all know how they love complicated, multiple layers of bureaucracy. The government sets up a new Social Security plan for those of us born in 1969 and later (this includes me—I'm not like those people who tell you what you should do, all the while not being held to the same standards). We have the government mandate that every working American must plan for his or her own retirement and save or invest money for the future. The key to this is that they can't touch the money in these accounts, which we will now control, period. If we don't get that part, forget this entire idea. They can't be involved at all except for mandating that we do it.

This means they can't take them over, they can't bail them out, and they cannot legislate them into going broke. This is where we hold ourselves accountable and our government at bay.

This might seem scary to many of you, but when you consider that the stock market has returned 10 percent per year on average during any ten-year period you want to look at, it becomes much clearer why we should be invested in the market and not in a trust fund run by Uncle Sam.

One of the keys to making a system like Social Security work in the beginning was to make it mandatory. Well, unfortunately, the same applies to this idea. Now don't go getting huffy on me here, we already discussed how we don't use the systems already in place the way we should. This would just be another tool that you don't use if it is not made mandatory. Honestly, if we all put the maximum in our 401(k)s (which, by the way, happens to be 15 percent of our income; funny how Uncle Sam can have a great idea but screw it up) we wouldn't need Social Security for those folks in 401(k)s at all. As it is too many people believe that Social Security was designed as "retirement." It was not. It was designed to supplement the retirement you were supposed to create on your own and be there as a safety net for those who fell short.

Some people on the Left say we don't have the knowledge to invest properly. They say that without this knowledge we would be too open to the pitfalls of the investment world. The day trader phenomenon gives us evidence both ways. Many day traders, those people who literally attempt to make their living off of daily movement in the market, lose big money and eventually go back to work, while others seem to make the system work for them. Most of these people have no real training in what they are doing, and while some get lucky most do not. But we are not talking about working our retirement accounts like a day trader. We are talking about having well-rounded mutual funds and other securities that already have proven track records. I'll admit, I have about as much stock trading knowledge as I have igloo-building skills, which isn't much. But I do know that my own investments over the last year have done better than most, and this has only been because I looked at my risk and return with my advisor. That's right, my advisor—a trained professional in the business, not an elected politician. You hear that part? *With my advisor.* The plan I am suggesting doesn't force you to go it alone, it just forces you to go it without government. I would not give up the ability to use any tool at my disposal in helping me make the call on a stock or fund. I have a great advisor, and while you would not be forced to use one, and while there is some cost involved with using one, I think most of us would be fools not to use one.

So what happens if we go to a system like this and we don't follow through? Why make it mandatory? On that part of the plan I agree with the questioning, and it's my plan! I'm not committed to that part all that strongly, but I fear that if it is not mandatory many may not get into the program and then who will have to take care of them when retirement comes a-calling? That would be you and me.

I don't know about the rest of you, but my motivating factor for even writing this book has always been my kids. As I watch my parents in retirement I am so proud of them for what they achieved, especially considering they didn't really start planning their retirement until they were in their fifties. They went out of their way to provide my sisters and me with everything we had growing up, and as soon as they were done raising us they turned that same attention to their own retirement to ensure that we would not have to take care of them while raising our own children. The fact that we don't have to worry about them financially is a great gift from them. They know full well, however, that if the day comes they ever need financial assistance, all three of us would be there in a heartbeat to help. My parents have the ultimate retirement plan: They raised their kids up to be successful, they took care of their own needs for retirement, and they know we will all be there for them when and if the time comes that they need help. That's how you do it, folks.

This is what I want for my kids down the road, to not have to be burdened by my wife and me because of poor planning on our part. So really, what is the best way for us to ensure this gift to our kids?

By now the answer should be obvious. It has been estimated that for Social Security to continue in its present form into the next generation (that's us getting checks, folks) the average American could see as high as 70 percent of their income going in the form of taxes to keep the system fully funded. I looked at one of my pay stubs recently and found that 25.3 percent of my check goes to some form of taxation already. This is before the sales tax, property tax, gasoline tax, and every other tax we have to pay. In the end we pay between 42 and 48 percent of our income in taxes of some kind. So with 70 percent of their income taken in taxes, what are my kids going to have to save? This is disgusting to me and it should be to you, too.

Only by reducing the burden on the system are we doing anyone any good. And only by changing the system to allow us to provide for ourselves can we get this country back on track financially.

So we can take care of ourselves. Now, how do we keep the promise to the people like my folks who are already on Social Security and how do we take care of those who were born before 1969?

First of all, it is far from impossible. This is America—we put a man on the moon in less than a decade, we won the Second World War after getting sucker punched, and we have been the engine behind nearly every major advancement in mankind's history over the last two hundred years. We can figure this out together.

Some people suggest raising the cap on the SSI tax from your income. As it sits right now, you only pay SSI taxes on the first $106,000 that you earn. Eliminating the cap and making the tax apply to all the money earned as income would affect only the top income earners (you remember them, the people paying over 34.27 percent of all income taxes anyway). The Left calls this "paying their fair share," but what is fair about carrying the load for everyone else? We will talk about that later.

Who are these people that would be affected by the changes in taxes for Social Security? Are they the super rich? Not even close. The top income earners in this country, the top 1 percent, are any couples making more than $295,495 per year. Not exactly the mega-rich *Forbes* 500 types.

Some others suggest tiers within the tax system. Something like taxing the first $106,000 of every million made, but that is a stupid idea because most people who are part of the top 1 percent of income earners don't make millions. These plans all rally around one central idea, raising taxes as a means of punishing the high-income earners in the country, and that's just stupid.

What we should be doing is looking at where the money goes that Uncle Sam does get. We need to cut spending (really cut spending, not just cut proposed increases like the government does from time to time while screaming that the sky is falling), and we need to cut it now more than ever. President Obama's wild spending increases are only going to make this harder to deal with. First we cut all spending by 10 percent today, and I mean every line item, including military spending. The only ones we do not touch are veteran's benefits and Social Security benefits for those born before 1969. These people have given so much; we have no right to take it away. But in the future the increases in spending will have to be more targeted.

Next we call in the auditors to look into every government-run program in existence. This is the evaluation process. What we are looking for here is waste. From eighteen federal employees to do the jobs of twelve to financing the arts, we start making real cuts and eliminating programs that have either made no difference or have been so poorly managed that in the private sector they would have gone out of business. Scary thing about this idea is that *a lot* of programs do not even meet the lowest bar of success and would need to be scrapped. But if we are taking the people born after 1969 out of the system and requiring them to manage their own retirement accounts, we would have to do something drastic. As I said earlier, we put a man on the moon and split the atom, so we can do this. We just have to get the politics out of it and concentrate on the people. Once we get through the baby boomers, the rest is a cakewalk as you will control your destiny and the country will be much better off.

Let's take a few minutes and look at one of the programs that will either need to be scrapped or at least undergo some major overhauls. The time has come for us to really evaluate the Welfare programs in this country. Aside from the direct cost to taxpayers there is the lost revenue from those people in the system and the perpetual generational damage it does to our society.

Today the number of people collecting Welfare checks is about half of what it was in 1996. I give credit to both political parties for this accomplishment—the Republicans for writing the bill and President Clinton for signing it. But the time has come to truly revamp this system to include some upward mobility to it, not just the bread-and-water techniques of the Great Society.

Too many people assisted by social welfare programs in this country are trapped by the very programs that were intended to help them. I'm not taking a shot at the people in the program at this point, just making an honest observation of the situation.

Let's look at all the "good" LBJ's Great Society has done. According to the US Census Bureau, throughout the 1970s, 1980s, and 1990s the system "helped" a large number of people. When Welfare started in its current incarnation, about 2 percent of the US population was receiving some kind of public assistance. It grew steadily throughout the decades until it finally hit something of a critical mass. In 1996 the Republicans in Congress took aim and came up with reforms that were designed to bring people out of the Welfare roles and get them back to work. Well, I am happy to report that today about 2 percent of the US population is receiving some kind of public assistance.

Can you see the problem here? In 1970 there were 203,000,000 people in the United States and 2 percent, or 4,060,000, of them were on public assistance. The great success of this program that was supposed put an end to poverty still has 2 percent of a nation (estimated to now be 305,000,000 people) on Welfare. That means today there are 6,100,000 people receiving taxpayer money. This does not appear to be a reduction in poverty. Yet it is touted as a success. Only in government circles can an increase of over 50 percent be seen as a success, even though the goal was an elimination of poverty. Hell, I would have been happy with a 50 percent reduction in the number of people over fifty years because we know there will always be poor people. It's just a fact of life.

Here is how success manifests itself in our current Welfare program. Susan has been on Welfare for four years. She was a classic teen pregnancy. She dropped out of high school when she found out she was pregnant to work and raise her child. Unfortunately, with her lack of education she can only get a part-time job making minimum wage. But she is hungry to work and wants to make more money to support her child so she goes to night school (also provided by the public at no charge) and earns her GED. Susan has been receiving $500 a month in assistance, plus low-income housing. She earns, at this point, $1,200 per month, which means she is living on $1,700 per month. This puts her just over $20,000 per year.

Susan is a hard worker, makes good choices at work, and seems to understand the business. Her boss makes her assistant manager and she receives an increase of $200 per month, which should mean she's making $1,900 per month. But she does not. Uncle Sam finds out that Susan has worked hard and received a raise and to congratulate her he cuts her assistance by $200 per month. So in the end she has worked her butt off to increase her take-home pay by $0.00 per month, give or take.

Now in another year she makes store manager and is rewarded for her hard work with another $500 per month, bringing her off the Welfare roles completely and making her $1,900 per month or $22,800 per year. Over the five years of this process we have invested $26,700 in direct payments, the cost of running the night school she went to in order to get her GED, the balance of the low-cost housing she didn't have to pay for, WIC to help her give her child nutritional meals, possibly the cost of public transportation to get her to and from her job, and finally the healthcare for her child, from well-baby visits to immunizations and daycare. I did a rough estimate of what that costs and here's what I came up with:

Direct payments four years at $500/mth
+ one year at $300/mth . . . . . . . . . . . . . . . . . $26,700

Her portion of the night school and
public transportation. . . . . . . . . . . . . . . . . . . unknown

Half of her fictional $600/mth rent
for five years . . . . . . . . . . . . . . . . . . . . . . . . . $18,000

WIC (eggs, milk, and cheese
only for two for one year). . . . . . . . . . . . . . . . . .$337

Daycare for five years at $100 per week. . . . . $24,000

Healthcare from prenatal to the child
being five years old. . . . . . . . . . . . . . . . . . . $30,000*
*Assuming no complications during birth, a one-night
hospital stay, and a child of average birth weight.

Add that up and we are pushing the $100,000 number. So we, the American people, have invested $99,037 in Susan and her child and she is still on the verge of needing our help. Susan's $22,800 a year is now even more desperate because she now has to cover a larger portion of her rent, daycare, and groceries. So has she really made any progress? Sure she has, but where has the benefit been to us and why should she not feel a bit more secure? Because the system is broken. This is why people stay on Welfare for generations sometimes. This is why we still have 2 percent of Americans on public assistance. Another unintended circumstance following the very best of intentions or just another failure of the system to address the root causes of the problem?

Best part of all is this: Her child has now developed with a world experience that says poverty is the norm. Susan does not have to repay a cent of what we gave her and there is a very real chance that her child will grow up to need assistance also. She also has not paid taxes in five years and, if anything, has received the earned income credit for her low income, meaning you can add a few thousand dollars and easily push beyond $100,000.

This is an approximation of the system we have today. It is all well intentioned but if you look at the numbers it has done nothing to help the situation. In fact, I would suggest that it has gotten worse. Now this is not to say that it has not helped some. I'm sure there are plenty of stories of families who have broken the cycle of poverty and come out the other side, thankful that it was there to assist them. My point is that there should be more of those stories and less Susan stories. In nearly fifty years we have experienced a six trillion dollar transfer of wealth through this system. Yet we have more people accessing the system than when it started, which means no matter how you want to compare it, the system has failed.

So I put my thinking cap on and thought about what I would want if I were in a situation where I needed assistance. I would want three things:
1) Freedom
2) Independence
3) Security

So around these three core beliefs, the same ones I apply to everything I do, I put together a plan that I believe would work, save the country money, bring security to the people in need, ultimately bring independence, and bring the freedom of self-determination.

So let's revisit Susan again from the start. A classic teen mother she contemplates dropping out of school. Step one in the Average American Self-Assistance Plan (AASAP) is she cannot quit school. She must stay in school if we are going to invest in her future. As for the others, they can go it alone, but if they choose that route they need to understand that certain steps will need to be taken before they can receive assistance when they come back. And they will only come back if they are ready to earn what they get.

Under AASAP Susan would enlist (a military term for a reason) for four years. During this time she will receive $36,000 per year, paid directly to her in the form of preprinted checks already made out to the debt holders, in her case the school tuition she will pay, the rent she will pay, utility bills she will pay, the child care she will pay, the medical insurance she will pay into (either a government plan or private insurer), another check for the savings she will have to put away for emergencies (10 percent), and the balance directed into her checking account. During this time she will also be required to study for her high school equivalency exam, which can be pursued at the same time she is studying in her classes for the vocation or degree of her choice. These preprinted checks only last for the first two years, until she has a real handle on her expenses, then the total goes into her checking. At the end of this first twenty-four-month period she will have $7,200 in savings and a solid track record of managing her money. At this point of the process the American people can reevaluate how the program has worked to date and tweak it as needed.

With two years under her belt she is on track to becoming whatever she wants and the money will continue for two more years. What has she gained just in the first two years? Well, it's not just her but her child as well. The child has seen the importance of education, has enjoyed a mother with some pride that she is taking care of her child, and the respect others will show them both knowing that she is doing the right thing to eventually break the cycle. Little Johnny or Janet has had two birthdays where Mom was able to shop for him/her with money she saved.

Over the next two years she will manages the cash flow in and out completely with the help of financial advisors hired from the private sector on her behalf. We organize with private companies to cover the cost of this with their understanding that they are encouraging the next two generations of shoppers who will buy their wares and increase their market share.

The final two years come to pass and we have a well-trained, educated, proud individual who knows she can take care of herself, her child, and her future. We also have a taxpayer who will now reinvest into the programs through her payroll taxes.

We also have accomplished breaking the cycle for her child as they both now value the educational process and we have quite possibly eliminated the second generation from ever needing assistance. The hope is that as each four-year period comes to pass the spending can be reduced, not increased, as it is needed less and less. I am not an idiot, it will never go away, but it should be able to shrink to a manageable level within a generation or approximately twenty-four years.

So we have a real objective with a time limit so we can really tell whether it has produced results. We have fewer and fewer people in need of the program and it requires less money for us to fund every year after the initial four years of it running, and we have truly measurable results. We have also saved millions, perhaps billions, from the generational effects of poverty. Now might be a good time to see what the actual definition of *conservative* is. The *American Heritage Dictionary* defines the noun *conservative* as: one favoring traditional views and values.

What could be more traditional than having people take pride in their ability to provide for themselves while sharing the values of self-determination in a country as free as the United States of America?

What about the cost? Good question. As we established earlier there are approximately 6.1 million people on assistance right now in the US. Welfare alone, in all its different disguises, costs us approximately 37 percent of the federal budget not counting Social Security. So of the $2,600,000,000,000 that we spend in total in 2009, $962,000,000,000 is on Welfare-related programs. With a total of forty-three million people accessing varying degrees of assistance we are spending an average of $22,372 per person already, and we have no end in sight. My plan would cost us $878,000,000,000 over four years, not one. That's only $219,000,000,000 per year for the first four with reductions each year after that. We could well cut it in half within the first twenty-four years and save ourselves enough money to pay off the national debt in just 16.5 years. I'm not talking about having a budget surplus; I'm talking about being out of debt as a nation for the first time since January 8, 1835, when the debt was zero. Those are real dollars that our government would no longer have to tax us for because they would no longer need the money.

Now, I understand that conservatives are pegged as wanting to keep things the same and not wanting change, but that is change I could get behind and I am willing to bet many conservatives could, too. And it would even allow for my 10 percent cut in all federal spending in the first year as nearly $600,000,000 would be available to fund Social Security as I said we must.

So we have managed in just the first few pages to pay off the national debt, reduce the cost of Social Security on future generations while allowing those people to fund their own retirement, reduce the number of people on Welfare, increase the number of taxpayers, and reduce the overall cost of government, which in turn reduces the government's need for unlimited funds taken from you and me. And we are just getting started.

# *Chapter 2*

The Constitution of the United States has been usurped, leading the states to take on a secondary role in governance and responsibility to the masses. Cases in point: education and infrastructure.

Education, according to the Constitution, is the sole right and responsibility of the many states, yet today the federal government has taken control of our schools through extortion. If the states do not offer certain classes or provide these classes in accordance with the federal government's requirements, financial aid for education will be affected. This covers everything from sex education to score-rating systems to final exit examinations designed in partnership with the federal government. In addition, the federal government has ceded a percentage of its power to the teachers' unions who have as their main interest the teachers and not the students.

The infrastructure of the United States of America, while being the financial responsibility of the states through the various departments of transportation in each state, is dictated to a major degree by the federal funds available to each state. These funds from the federal coffers are awarded based on a number of criteria, ranging from requirements that the states recognize federal holidays to the speed limits in each state.

As we have already seen, the federal government is not suited to be too deeply involved in too many things. So why do we allow *our* federal government to collect the money we need for our local roads, bridges, and educations?

Let's look at infrastructure first then we will delve into education.

We should look first to the Constitution to see what it says about infrastructure, roads, bridges, and even our electrical grid. I'll give you a minute to research that. The Constitution is printed in the back of this book for your convenience.

Oh, good, I see you're back. You found what I did: nothing.

So why are they in charge of it? Let's be clear about this, our government had and continues to have a vested interest in our highway system for the moving of military equipment, men, and supplies across the huge land. This is why in the 1950s there was a concerted effort to build our amazing interstate highway system. In fact, President Eisenhower once said that he considered the building of the interstate highway system the greatest accomplishment of his presidency. I would have to agree. Although I believe that had the states decided to build it, this system could have been done, it may well have been done faster thanks to governmental intervention. But here is where the system went haywire. The monies used to maintain this system should be left to the many states to use as they deem necessary. I have no issue with the federal government mandating that these highways need to be maintained, but they do not need to collect the funds to do so. Every time the federal government collects money for the states and local governments it takes a piece of it in the process. This is because of the administration of the program at the federal level. This is the case with every single section of our economy where the Feds have a say in the collection of resources. That's what tax dollars are: resources.

Then when the money gets to the state there is another group of administrators who have to be paid, their buildings must be paid for, the insurance carried on the building must be paid for,

and the money must be doled out to the support staff. If it is a
local program that the money gets collected for, you now have
yet another layer of administrators with another set of overhead
expenses that have to be met.

Look at it as a family structure. Let's say that your great-
grandparents have all the money in your family and each
generation down the line is another layer of government.
Great-Grandpa is the federal government, your grandpa is
the state government, your dad is the county government,
and you are the city government. Great-Grandpa mandated
(passed a law) requiring you to maintain (mow) the lawn.
He collects the money to run the lawn mower and collects
$10. He now takes a dollar out of that money and sends $9 to
your grandpa (the state). Grandpa decides that since he owns
the mower at the state level that it must be run on supreme
unleaded gas. To monitor this he installs meters around the
yard (state) to check exhaust and takes $2 from the $9 for his
processing and monitoring (law enforcement) and sends the
remainder to your dad (the county). Your dad collects the $7
and now has to account for the fact that your brother needs
to go to school. So he has to fuel up his car to take him, but
Grandpa stopped paying for that last month. But Dad already
promised it (another entitlement program that has nothing
to do with mowing the lawn, mind you) to your brother. So
Dad takes $1 for his processing and distribution costs and
another $1 for this other program previously canceled by
Grandpa (the state) but that was already promised to your
brother (another city). Now you receive $5 to mow the lawn.
But, surprise, you have to buy the gas for it, the expensive
gas mandated by Grandpa (the state), and you have to make
the run to the school to drop off your brother (another city)
because Dad (the county) forgot he didn't have time to do it
that day. So now what should have taken you a half hour to do
and made you $5 now costs you $3 for gas in the mower and
another half hour out of your day because of your brother's
need to get to school.

This seems simplistic, but it is what is happening every day in America and not just to the $10 we send them but to hundreds of billions of dollars every year.

The fact is that the states and local governments have the necessary mechanisms in place to raise the needed taxes to run these programs at the local levels. Not to mention the constitutionality of the situation that flies in the face of it. Let's see …

Let us start where we always should; we need to look at the Constitution itself. It is broken down into seven articles. Article 1 has ten sections, which are listed in the back of this book as is the entire Constitution and the Bill of Rights. This first article lists what Congress shall have the power to do. Article 2 deals with the executive branch and is broken down into four sections. Article 3 addresses the Supreme Court. Article 4 focuses on the relationship between the federal and state governments and our relationship with the federal government as free persons. Article 5 discusses the rules under which the Constitution can be altered. Article 6 concentrates on the Oath of Office and the importance of us operating as a singular country and that the Law of the Land shall be prescribed by the Constitution and no state law can go against it. And Article 7 covers the ratification process of the Constitution itself.

So maybe we can shed some light on this subject using Article 4, which addresses the relationship between us and our government and the states and the federal government. Article 4 is reproduced in the following:

**Article. IV.**

*Section. 1.*

Full Faith and Credit shall be given in each State to the public Acts, Records, and judicial Proceedings of every other State. And the Congress may by general Laws prescribe the Manner in which such Acts, Records and Proceedings shall be proved, and the Effect thereof.

*Section. 2.*

Clause 1: The Citizens of each State shall be entitled to all Privileges and Immunities of Citizens in the several States.

Clause 2: A Person charged in any State with Treason, Felony, or other Crime, who shall flee from Justice, and be found in another State, shall on Demand of the executive Authority of the State from which he fled, be delivered up, to be removed to the State having Jurisdiction of the Crime.

Clause 3: No Person held to Service or Labour in one State, under the Laws thereof, escaping into another, shall, in Consequence of any Law or Regulation therein, be discharged from such Service or Labour, but shall be delivered up on Claim of the Party to whom such Service or Labour may be due . . .

*Section. 3.*

Clause 1: New States may be admitted by the Congress into this Union; but no new State shall be formed or erected within the Jurisdiction of any other State; nor any State be formed by the Junction of two or more States, or Parts of States, without the Consent of the Legislatures of the States concerned as well as of the Congress.

Clause 2: The Congress shall have Power to dispose of and make all needful Rules and Regulations respecting the Territory or other Property belonging to the United States; and nothing in this Constitution shall be so construed as to Prejudice any Claims of the United States, or of any particular State.

*Section. 4.*

The United States shall guarantee to every State in this Union a Republican Form of Government, and shall protect each of them against Invasion; and on Application of the Legislature, or of the Executive (when the Legislature cannot be convened) against domestic Violence.

Well, I didn't see anything about the Fed having to collect money for the states, did you? I didn't think so. It seems we may have to look elsewhere to find where the federal government derives its authority to run the daily activities of the states. Maybe the Bill of Rights has something:

- First Amendment: Freedom of Speech
- Second Amendment: Right to Bear Arms
- Third Amendment: Conditions for Quartering Soldiers
- Fourth Amendment: Right or Searches and Seizure Regulated
- Fifth Amendment: Rights in Prosecution
- Sixth Amendment: Right to a Speedy Trial
- Seventh Amendment: Right to Trial by Jury
- Eighth Amendment: No Excessive Bail or Cruel Treatment
- Ninth Amendment: Rule of Construction of the Constitution
- Tenth Amendment: Rights Reserved to the States

Anyone see the right of the federal government to collect funds for the states? I sure didn't. But what I do see is that last right, the Tenth Amendment, and it makes me wonder if there might not be an answer in there. Let's check it out a little closer.

The Tenth Amendment: The powers not delegated to the United States by the Constitution, nor prohibited by it to the States, are reserved to the States respectively, or to the people.

Huh? That almost reads like it is up to the state to do any of the things not mentioned in the Constitution or the Bill of Rights. That might even apply to the highway systems in this country, now wouldn't it?

So why would we need a Department of Transportation? Or a Department of Education, for that matter? These two departments take up a pretty big piece of the budget pie for the Feds. Transportation will get an estimated $73,450,000,000 in 2010, according to http://www.gpoaccess.gov/usbudget/fy10/

bis.html, and education will get another $97,285,000,000, according to the same site. That's, let me see ... 97 billion dollars plus 73 billion dollars, carry the one . . . holy crap: $170,000,000,000. And that's just for one year. Imagine $170 billion going back to the states every year for the next ten years. For those states strapped for cash, 1.7 trillion dollars would sure come in handy.

The other major place in which local governments have been shoved aside is in education. Almost $100 billion dollars will move through the federal government's hands in the next year on its way back to the states. The federal government employs 16 percent of the United States today. That's a hell of a lot more than GM, Ford, Chrysler, Sears, IBM, Microsoft, GE, and Wal-Mart combined. In a country of three hundred million people that's like hiring all of California (36,000,000), Nevada (2,600,000), Arizona (6,500,000), and New Mexico (2,000,000) and still having about two hundred thousand jobs to fill. And this is paid for with over $9,000 per student on average plus the overhead at the federal level. Why? What are we getting for our federal bucks? Not very good education, that is for darn sure. Why is it not possible for the states to run their own education? Let's look into what the federal government did to usurp power in this area.

Standardized test scores had been steadily going down in the United States since the start of the Cold War. In fact, today's students do not even come close to scoring as students did in the first ten years of the twentieth century, one hundred years ago. But it was at the start of the Cold War, the 1950s, that the federal government started laying the groundwork to usurp the states' authority on education. First thing the Feds had to do was up the ante on the importance of education to a federal level. This was done in the early 1950s by Republican President Eisenhower. Eisenhower created the Department of Health, Education, and Welfare. "The purpose of this plan is to improve the administration of the vital health, education, and social security functions now being carried on in the Federal Security Agency by giving them departmental rank" (Eisenhower, March 12, 1953).

I know, many of you thought this was a vast left-wing conspiracy, but it wasn't. Have you ever heard the term "A tiger does what a tiger does"? It means that when a tiger turns and eats its trainer, it's just doing what a tiger does, killing to eat. Well, government works in much the same way. The constant expansion of government for the benefit of government is just what government does. It was one of the things we were most warned about by our Founding Fathers.

> "Government is not reason; it is not eloquence. It is force. And force, like fire, is a dangerous servant and a fearful master" (George Washington). "Government, even in its best state, is but a necessary evil; in its worst state, an intolerable one" (Thomas Paine). "When once a republic is corrupted, there is no possibility of remedying any of the growing evils but by removing the corruption and restoring its lost principles; every other correction is either useless or a new evil" *(Thomas Jefferson)*.

These are but a few of the quotes attributed to some of our Founding Fathers. Learned beyond their years, they saw clearly that which we now have to deal with: A government that has swollen, like a river beyond its banks, and must be contained.

Anyway, after the new loftier status of education came more pressure to perform. By the late 1950s it was already being realized that standardized test scores were dropping. So the government's answer to this was, of course, more government. Along came more legislation, namely, the National Defense Education Act (NDEA), which was launched as much in response to Russia launching Sputnik as to the falling test scores. Then in the 1960s came Title IV of the Civil Rights Act, Title IX of the Education Amendments of 1972, and Section 504 of the Rehabilitation Act of 1973, which prohibited discrimination based on race, sex, or disability. Now the government was cooking with fire. They had officially set the stage for a full-scale takeover of education based on discrimination. Keep in mind that the states were every bit as competent as the federal government to manage the new and emerging laws, but because of a few backward states like Alabama and other far Southern states, the Feds were able to justify in their own minds what they needed to do. It was at this point that every state in the Union should have been jumping up and down and screaming from the rafters to stop this federal overreach, but to the dismay of really nobody, they didn't. Our parents and grandparents were busy working and as the 1970s dragged on and the recessionary pressures of the Carter administration wore away people's earning potential through higher interest rates and higher energy prices, gas, heating oil, and the like, people were too focused on their immediate needs to pay much attention to what Uncle Sam was doing and about to do.

Enter the peanut farmer and the full-scale squat lift to full cabinet position of education. The year was 1980 and James Carter, the fortieth president of the United States, was about as clueless as they come, but he stayed on script. Standardized test scores had continued to fall year by year with few exceptions and the Department of Education was poised to gain a real seat at the table of power. Congress, at Carter's urging, created the Department of Education officially and made it a full cabinet position within the President's Cabinet. Now they (the Department of Education) had a real voice. And what did they do with that voice? They asked for more money and more money and more money. A tiger does what a tiger does.

As we know, every coin has two sides. The education coin does as well. But where you might believe that the other side of the coin is us or the local schools, in this case it is the teachers' union, the National Education Association (NEA). As I mentioned earlier, this is where much of that federal power is vested today. The NEA has so much sway over legislators that it is scary. When President Bush passed No Child Left Behind (NCLB) with Ted Kennedy's assistance it was partially for cover from the NEA. Kennedy, a strong proponent of unions and the NEA in particular, was Bush's saving grace in this fight for America's children. Although the NEA fought it every step of the way from the first time Bush mentioned it during the 2000 campaign, Kennedy undoubtedly served as cover to some degree from the fire-breathing educators.

Once passed, the NEA did its level best to bring up every shortcoming of the plan over the next several years, even going so far as to claim that it was underfunded from the start. But it wasn't. All the money appropriated for the program was doled out as promised. So the NEA went to battle with the program right from the start. In 2005 the NEA sued to get more funding for NCLB, which is weird considering their initial stance on the program. They requested a doubling of the spending from a little over $12,000,000,000 to $28,000,000,000. According to the *Deseret News* of Salt Lake City:

> And once it was enacted, the union continued its opposition, using the argument that not enough money was put behind the law to allow it to be effectively implemented. It is a charge that has been taken up by Democrats in Congress and one that was used against Bush by Democratic presidential nominee Sen. John Kerry in the 2004 campaign. In the third Bush–Kerry debate last October in Tempe, Ariz., the Democratic candidate said, "The president who talks about No Child Left Behind refused to fully fund—by $28 billion—that particular program so you can make a difference in the lives of those young people. . . . The president reneged on his promise to fund No Child Left Behind."
>
> That $28 billion Kerry mentioned is the shortfall figure the NEA uses in its argument now. It's not a coincidence. In the 2004 campaign, the NEA spent $1.16 million to fund ads, mailings and other activities to defeat Bush. Many of the ads attacked No Child Left Behind.
>
> At their annual convention last July in Washington, NEA members were urged by Weaver and other union leaders to host 'house parties' before the November elections to build opposition to a law that "forces us to

spend money we don't have, on programs we don't need, to get test results that don't matter."

"NEA also spent another $235,000 on behalf of Kerry. Kerry and the NEA have long been close friends and allies. The union endorsed Kerry in 2004. Moreover, the NEA spent more than $1.6 million on the 2004 congressional elections, the vast majority of it, 91 percent, on behalf of Democratic candidates."

So basically the NEA lied. The 28 billion dollar figure was never the proposed spending for the program. Perhaps the scariest part is the way Democrats, sitting members of our government, took the NEA's numbers and ran with them. This is the clearest indication of who is making education policy in this country. Not our elected officials but the teachers' unions.

Some of you will think you have caught me in a hypocritical moment here. I am a strong proponent of keeping the smartest people on a subject involved in the policy making for that segment of our country. Take oil exploration, for example. I want the oil companies in the conversation about drilling for oil and here is why, *they are successful at it*. Even in light of the recent BP disaster, when viewed against how many billions of barrels they have brought up safely, they still represent the most knowledgeable group on the subject. Does that make sense? If the teachers' union were turning out kids who were testing near the top globally, if there were increasingly higher test scores for math, science, reading, and writing, I would be all for their input on educational issues. You've seen what happens when government doesn't get input from experts on moneymaking and wealth building; we are, as a country, broke. Not only are we broke, but we are carrying over ten trillion dollars in debt. That's $10,000,000,000,000.

But what other leverage did the government use to gain control over education? Well, they used good old-fashioned scare tactics and facts because facts can be made to say a lot of things. Between 1972 and 1980, SAT scores were on the decline.

## Average SAT Scores, 1972–2005

| | Verbal Score | | | Mathematical Score | | |
|------|------|--------|-------|------|--------|-------|
| Year | Male | Female | Total | Male | Female | Total |
| 1972 | 531 | 529 | 530 | 527 | 489 | 509 |
| 1976 | 511 | 508 | 509 | 520 | 475 | 497 |
| 1980 | 506 | 498 | 502 | 515 | 473 | 492 |
| 1984 | 511 | 498 | 504 | 518 | 478 | 497 |
| 1988 | 512 | 499 | 505 | 521 | 483 | 501 |
| 1990 | 505 | 496 | 500 | 521 | 483 | 501 |
| 1992 | 504 | 496 | 500 | 521 | 484 | 501 |
| 1994 | 501 | 497 | 499 | 523 | 487 | 504 |
| 1996 | 507 | 503 | 505 | 527 | 492 | 508 |
| 1998 | 509 | 502 | 505 | 531 | 496 | 512 |
| 2000 | 507 | 504 | 505 | 533 | 498 | 514 |
| 2002 | 507 | 502 | 504 | 534 | 500 | 516 |
| 2004 | 512 | 504 | 508 | 537 | 501 | 518 |
| 2005 | 513 | 505 | 508 | 538 | 504 | 520 |

As you can see from the table, the average SAT verbal score was dropping pretty quickly, as were SAT mathematical scores. Now, the SATs are those wonderful tests you take at the end of high school that assess you for college admittance. While we have recovered in math (but barely, we should be thirty years ahead in testing if they, the government, was going to fix everything), we still lag far behind in where we were with verbal communication in 1972. In fact, after the 1980 creation of the Department of Education we continued to drop like a rock in verbal until the late 1990s. If you have talked to a teenager in the past ten years you would believe *um* is a word. So, again I ask you, why would we be gaining insight from a bunch of teachers or their union on education, especially considering their rate of "success"?

Other test scores were also dropping in the 1970s. Reading scores dropped just as dramatically and have yet to recover. Even with the intervention of Uncle Sam into education we have not seen a full recovery from the 1980s test scores as a whole. That's thirty years of substandard assistance from the federal government.

This is how they took it over. They convinced many in the electorate (that's you and me and our congressmen) that we were too stupid to run the education system in this country. Too often our local elected officials just went along with it instead of returning to what had worked in the past. Local control, local input; that is what had been missing since the 1950s. Yet we allowed the government to *usurp* that control away from us.

But it gets better. The government then started spending money in addition to the money we still raised locally on education. Property taxes are the most common way of raising money for schools but block grants from Uncle Sam are also available. The only problem with that is this is money that should have been raised locally and given directly to the school districts. The most local level of control over any governmental agency is the most effective. We now spend an average of over $9,000 in this country per student per year. That is higher that any other industrialized country in the world, yet we place around twentieth in our overall ranking in education. As President Bush once asked, "Is our kids learning?" Nice example ... The answer is *no*. Or at least not as well as they should be learning.

From the Heritage Foundation:
Many people believe that lack of funding is a problem in public education, but historical trends show that American spending on public education is at an all-time high. Between 1994 and 2004, average per-pupil expenditures in American public schools have increased by 23.5 percent (adjusted for inflation). Between 1984 and 2004, real expenditures per pupil increased by 49 percent. These increases follow the historical trend of ever-increasing real per-student

expenditures in the nation's public schools. In fact, the per-pupil expenditures in 1970–1971 ($4,060) were less than half of per-pupil expenditures in 2005–2006 ($9,266) after adjusting for inflation.

So how is it that we can spend more and get less for our money? It's simple really: The federal government is ill equipped to handle education.

It has been said that for evil to triumph, good men must do nothing. Well, for government to grow, citizens need only do nothing.

So, how did they get their hands on this much money without anyone noticing that they had no authority under the Constitution to do so? We let them.

It's kind of hard to explain but to put it simply, we knew, or at least our representatives in the Congress and the White House knew. So did the states. This is why I use the word *usurped* when discussing what happened. *Usurped* means: "to seize and hold (a position, office, power, etc.) by force or without legal right; to use without authority or right; employ wrongfully; to commit forcible or illegal seizure of an office, power, etc.; encroach. To take the place of (another) without legal authority; supplant." Dictionary.com.

And it is here in the last definition that we really get the impact of the word. "To take the place of (another) without legal authority; supplant." Now, the only way to do that is if the person or entity being usurped does not put up a fight. Welcome to the nightmare America. Our politicians at the state and federal levels didn't put up much of a fight, and we the American people sure as hell didn't get around to doing it.

When we elect people to represent us we tend to think our job is over. "We sent good men and women up to Capitol Hill and they will look out for us." This would be great if it were the case all the time. And while it is the case sometimes, in a lot of cases we send a person up there who for the next two or six years (Senate seats are held for six years, not two like the House of Representatives) spends a good amount of their time on the campaign trail, especially the last eighteen months before the election. Oh no, you don't! The process to get into office and serve a six-year term is almost an eight-year project. I'm not sure about you, but my mind changes on a lot of issues over an eight-year period and many of my feelings change precisely because of what I see happening in Washington. This is why electing people with a solid core matters. Imagine people in Boston who have had the same senator since before I was born. For the last forty-five years Ted Kennedy had been in the Senate representing Massachusetts. And somehow, every six years he had managed to convince enough voters he had changed just enough to keep up with the times. This is an excellent argument for term limits. If it's good enough for the president why is it not good enough for Congress? Three terms for the House of Representatives and two for the Senate would do nicely.

So again, who was supposed to be watching the store while the federal government took control? You were and I was and our parents and grandparents were.

How do we take back control of our government and get them out of the business of doing things for the states that they are more than capable of doing themselves?

First of all, we vote for the candidate that most meets with our expectation of what should be going on in Washington. Second, we don't rest on that as being our only civic duty. We need to get up and get out. Go to your local congressional representative's office when they are home on break, e-mail them and call them, send them faxes in order to make sure that he or she knows what your point of view is on a particular subject. Do the same with your local government. Go to a town council meeting and show up in person at a county meeting. When you find out that a presidential hopeful will be in your town, go see them. Ask a question that matters to you from the audience, and if they screen the questions raise hell about it.

More importantly, if you think you can help or change the situation for the better, run for office yourself. Throw your name in the hat. Many of us know plenty of people with whom we agree on many subjects. If you are a good writer or a good speaker get out there and let your natural talents lend a hand to your cause, whatever it may be. We all have a built-in number of associates who know somebody who can put us in touch with someone else who can help us run for office. Thanks to President Obama, we all now know that with as little formal training as a community organizer you can become president just four short years after winning your first national office. So why not try? I hear the benefits are out of this world.

Now some of you are probably thinking, "If it doesn't work as designed, why not change it back?" Well, if it was that easy I would not have had to write a book about how to do it.

First of all, you now have entrenched at the federal level thousands of employees who do what federal employees do; they try to maintain the need for their job. As the Heritage Foundation reported, "These funds were spent by 13 federal departments and multiple agencies." Did you get that? A total of thirteen different agencies in the federal government hand this money out. That's a lot of government employees trying to protect their government jobs. And we all know how well government employees communicate with each other.

It will take real leadership to dethrone these people and move them back into the economy where they can produce something. We won't be able to do anything about it if we don't get this economy going in the right direction; otherwise, we will just be putting people out of work to put people out of work.

But wait, if the schools have the additional money coming directly to them instead of Uncle Sam taking a portion to pay all these likely high-paid individuals to dole it out, perhaps they can get jobs … in the schools? It doesn't really matter all that much because less taxation going to Washington means more jobs will be created in the private sector for them in the end. That is a fact that has been proven three times in recent American history, under Kennedy, Reagan, and W. Bush.

Like I said, it will take leadership and a clear message. That message is simple: The federal government has failed to reach the objectives it outlined for the Department of Education. That's the simple message backed up by the facts.

# Chapter 3

Abortion should not be legislated.

While the decision to commit to having an abortion is a monumental undertaking for the mother, and in many cases the father, this is a subject that should be ignored by federal politicians entirely. The national state has absolutely no right to be involved in the debate. While it would be better if none were performed, this is a stand on which I believe most Americans can agree, it is intrusive of the government to take a position either for or against the procedure. This is a moral decision, an issue that should be debated solely within the church and in the family because the consequences will be felt by and dealt with by all involved, from the doctor who performs the procedure to the parents or parent making the decision. To clarify, I am speaking specifically about any and all abortions performed prior to the fetus's ability to survive beyond the confines of the womb. The inhumane act of partial-birth abortion, where the fetus is viable without the need for an amniotic environment, should be banned.

Let's dig in....

Abortion should not be legislated at the federal level. It should not be the government's role to decide the legality of the procedure; it should instead be left up to the communities themselves.

Now before you throw the book at me, allow me to explain my position more fully here. *Community*, as defined by the dictionary, means: "a social, religious, occupational, or other group sharing common characteristics or interests and perceived or perceiving itself as distinct in some respect from the larger society within which it exists" or "a social group of any size whose members reside in a specific locality, share government, and often have a common cultural and historical heritage." Let's look at two key words from each of these definitions: "characteristics" and "heritage."

Characteristic: "pertaining to, constituting, or indicating the character or peculiar quality of a person or thing; typical; distinctive." We start here with a simple idea, that the peculiar quality of man is that we don't kill our children. It is for most humans a given that when they have a child the parents will care for that child from birth or even before to the end result of adulthood. We know this to be true because we are all here reading this right now. Our parents came from a long line of people who did not kill their babies. Right?

Heritage: "something that comes or belongs to one by reason of birth; an inherited lot or portion." Now, I have done quite a bit of research for this book, but this was the oddest inquiry made thus far. Google the following term and see what you come up with: "People with a heritage of killing unborn children." What you will find is that there is not one mention of any tribe, any culture, any nationality in which the killing of unborn children is considered a cultural or heritage-related right of the family. It simply is not something that any culture on earth strives for, it is not something any culture is proud of, nor is it something that you will find an advocacy group for. Except for one: Planned Parenthood. But even that group does not show up when Googled in this way, and this is the only way I can think of that you could make a sound argument for the killing of the unborn. Something you will find is the number 47,282,293. This is the total number of abortions that have been performed in the United States since the 1973 Supreme Court decision on *Roe v. Wade* until March 20, 2006. Can you imagine for a moment what we have lost? Over forty-seven million Americans who have never been given the opportunity to develop into anything in this beacon of freedom on the planet. Americans who could have been anything; the doctor who cures AIDS may have been among them, the scientist who develops a clean-burning fuel source may have been among them, or the next Mother Teresa or Gandhi, saving the world's poor and comforting those suffering from God knows what disease. Maybe we have lost the kid who would have grown up to actually end war in the Middle East, or who could have come up with a plan for world peace, or better yet, the kid who was supposed to discover the new religion that all mankind could get behind. We definitely lost forty-seven million taxpayers who could have been paying in (at least some of them would have been taxpayer age by now) to prop up the sacred cow of liberalism, the Social Security program, thus saving Grandma from choosing between food and her medicine. Maybe all we lost was the next Bill Gates; you remember him, the guy who gave us this thing I wrote this book on and the means to use it for researching all this kind of stuff.

Then again, maybe we lost nothing. Maybe all we did was save ourselves from the next Hitler, the next Manson, or the next Andrea Yates. Either way, we will never have the chance to know because they're all dead. Sure would hate to get to Heaven or Zen or Shangri-la or that place Scientology is selling and find out that we killed the one guy who would have created the alternative fuel source to destroy Halliburton and Exxon, or the guy who would finally get rid of all the Republicans by making them finally understand the liberal viewpoint with his charisma and charm.

The fact is these babies never had the chance to be what they could have been; they were never given the opportunity to thrive in this country. We are not even talking about the number of babies killed worldwide due to the moral clarity we ourselves have exported around the world with newer, quicker ways to dispatch the unborn. I hear liberals say quite often, "Those people in third world countries are starving because they have too many children to feed. They need abortions to limit the number of mouths to feed." Or this one, and it has to be one of my favorites, "If you couldn't feed your baby, would you want another one to have to take care of and watch starve to death?" My answer to this is to look at the glass the other way around. I would not want to watch my child starve to death, nor would I want another child to feed if I were in this situation, so perhaps I would try real hard to not get pregnant in the first place. What I would want is condoms and other birth control products so my wife would not have to endure the pain of an abortion and I would not have to deal with the loss of that child myself. I would also want new technology so that I might be able to produce enough food and clean water so that I could feed the ones I had.

This is only part of the human cost of this oftentimes barbaric procedure. Think for a moment of all those women who are now forced to suffer the pains of their decision. Think of the men who had to sit in silence and watch as their child was "terminated" because they had no rights to defend their children. Oh, the human toll here is much higher than forty-seven million. Many men, and I consider them the lucky ones, were probably never informed of the decision that was being made on their behalf, so at least they do not have to deal with the very real pains associated with the loss of a child.

I know, at this point a bra-burning mama of the 1960s is thinking, "'child,' it's not a 'child,' it's tissue, nothing more. Who is this man to sit here and lecture me on my body and my right to do with it what I please? Just what does this male pig think he's doing trying to tell a woman what she can and can't do with her own body?"

Well, I am a man, that much is true, but I am not telling you what you can and cannot do with your body. I am just making you aware of the horrible cost associated with abortion. I am all for you having all the rights afforded any other human being in this country. What I am asking you to do is use them responsibly.

Abortion is not birth control; it is in fact the ending of a valuable life. It might not be valuable to you, but to someone out there waiting for a child to adopt it sure is. Birth control is really pregnancy control and this should be practiced by all women, and men for that matter, married or not who do not want a child. But once you get pregnant, it is no longer pregnancy control, it is ending a life. Along with that comes some very real issues; psychological, mental, physical, and even, oh yes, sometimes even spiritual issues that will have to be dealt with by the mother, the father, and even the doctor performing the "procedure."

Sidebar—"procedure," isn't that a wonderful way of explaining this? It's as if you went to the doctor to have your appendix taken out because it was causing you pain.

Please understand I am not trying to overturn *Roe v. Wade*; it is, at least for now, the law of the land. What I want you to come away with from this chapter is the realization that everything you do produces a consequence. For many, the consequences of having an abortion are problems with friends and family, keeping a relationship going with the father, and getting on with a new relationship with another man after having gone through a "procedure" like this. Sometimes it can be even worse. The suicide rate for postabortion women is approximately thirty-five per one hundred thousand women, versus twenty per one hundred thousand suffering from a miscarriage and just six per one hundred thousand who have given live birth. Live birth situations actually produce a lower suicide rate than those for women who kill themselves who are not pregnant, running in at twelve per one hundred thousand. This information came from www.pregnantpause.org. This site also notes some interesting facts on suicide rates worldwide, which range from 1 to 4 percent in Europe and the US to 15 percent in Scandinavian countries. The site points out that this is not proof that abortion causes suicide. Looking at the stats, I find it hard to believe anyone can possibly come away from them without coming to the conclusion that abortion certainly does not lower the rate of suicide. In the interest of full disclosure, this site is run by people who are pro-life. Some have religious backgrounds and are putting this information out for purely religious reasons. So what? They have a right to make their case just as those who are pro-abortion do.

If this was a war like the one in Iraq, about which we hear almost daily from Left-leaning radio hosts and on our TV in the evening that the death toll is too high, that we are losing lives for no reason, and that we should stop it at once, I am sure the liberal antilife groups would be backing me with everything they had at their disposal. But these children were not lost to a suicide bomber who didn't speak a lick of English, and these Americans were not killed by terrorists who have jealousy over our way of life. These Americans were killed by Americans. And not just any Americans, but by the one American who has a heritage of protecting their unborn child, their mother.

Now we can apply what we have learned to the problem. People in general do not show the characteristics that lead to killing their unborn children, nor does any society claim that it has by heritage the cultural belief that the killing of unborn children is a good thing. Now, if we bind this idea that people do not want to kill their children with the idea of community involvement we should, in a perfect world, come up with no abortions. But, alas, this world is not perfect so we need some kind of generalized rules to live by as a society. *Community*, as you remember, was also defined as "a social group of any size whose members reside in a specific locality, share government …" There it is; the word *government*. Many of you have been struggling with this word since seeing it in the definition a few pages ago and thought I had simply skipped it so as to not have to deal with the idea. Wrong again.

Our government has moved from the halls of Washington to the pulpit. This is a clear violation of separation of church and state despite the fact that there is no such thing in the US Constitution. True fact: Regardless of the First Amendments wording, which reads "Congress shall make no law respecting an establishment of religion, or prohibiting the free exercise thereof," it does not deem them enemies of each other. "Establishment of religion" in the sense of a religion of the United States as England has today with the official "Church of England" or "prohibition of religion" as the old Soviet Union once maintained are far different than the relationship envisioned by the founders of this country. Neither is a good blueprint for a safe environment for religion to flourish and neither can ever stifle the underground following of religious principle or living a life based on any religious text. What the founders hoped for was a free country where the beliefs of others would be respected if not encouraged and protected if not supported. This is part of the problem with our government getting involved in such matters as abortion.

Abortion is the major religious issue of our time. The founders hoped that religion would work in conjunction with the government on issues that involved morality over law enforcement. Now some of you are going to ask the question, "Where does he get that idea from?" I get it from the founders themselves.

From John Adams we hear this, "We have no government armed in power capable of contending in human passions unbridled by morality and religion. Our constitution was made only for a moral and religious people. It is wholly inadequate for the government of any other."

From Benjamin Franklin we hear these words, "I have lived, a long time, and the longer I live, the more convincing proofs I see of this truth—that God Governs in the affairs of men. And if a sparrow cannot fall to the ground without His notice, is it probable that an empire can rise without His aid?"

And from Alexander Hamilton we are told this, "In my opinion, the present constitution is the standard to which we are to cling.... Let an association be formed to be denominated 'The Christian Constitutional Society,' its object to be first: The support of the Christian religion. Second: The support of the United States."

There are more and I will cite them in a moment, but I believe it is important to focus on Alexander Hamilton's statement with a sharper view. Notice Hamilton does not charge religion with supporting the government first and foremost, but with supporting the Christian religion. This is clearly an example of the two working in conjunction while having different priorities. Religion is to be concerned foremost with the moral codes and spirituality of said religion and not on the actions of the government.

Separate they are to be, but not void of each other's knowledge and understanding as religion has as its second function the support of the spirituality of these United States in whatever fashion those believers see as appropriate so long as their dedication to their religion within the church is their primary focus and not government.

We move on to Patrick Henry, who gives us this quote, and please notice the order and by that the importance of each player in his mind in relation to the government. "The great pillars of all government ... [are] virtue, morality, and religion. This is the armor, my friend, and this alone, that renders us invincible." Religion, while mentioned, is listed last, indicating that its importance is clear, but that in government matters it is to be subservient to the will of the governed.

From Thomas Paine we learn this: "The cause of America is in a great measure the cause of all mankind. Where, say some, is the king of America? I'll tell you, friend, He reigns above." Although God's reign is unmatched in the lives of the people as he sits atop his throne in heaven, it is understood that the government is not going to be run by him, but by the men of this earth.

While there are many more that can be cited, and many to which the opposite can be inferred or straight-out read, it is in fact clear that to many of the Founding Fathers religion's role was to be in partnership with the government while not in direct support or opposition to the concept of a government of, by, and for the people. Both entities have their role to play in our country.

One last quote that, while short, clarifies for many the thinking of the forefathers en masse: "While just government protects all in their religious rights, true religion affords to government its surest support." George Washington said this, and again it clarifies the symbiotic relationship religion is to have with the state.

In fact, what most historians have said about the forefathers beliefs regarding religion is that they feared a dispute between dueling Christianities more than they feared Christianity making some claim on the seats of power in this country. By keeping a government free of official religion while maintaining that all religion should have its right to be freely exercised there was far less chance of upsetting one side or the other by means of keeping religion as a secondary support structure and not the primary guiding light of the government.

This brings us back to the abortion issue. It is a religious and moral issue far more than it is a question of our national sovereignty and security. As such it should be debated not in the halls of Congress but at the dinner tables of America. Let the churches lead the way on this subject as they change the hearts of men and women alike who are contemplating such extreme practices. But as such, we should not be comfortable with the government financially supporting either side of the discussion. Supporting Planned Parenthood and other organizations that profit from having the procedure done is not a good way to spend our money. It is, in fact, the subsidizing of our own demise.

# *Chapter 4*

The Tax Code and the Social Security Withholding of the United States of America should be completely rewritten.

The current code is too cumbersome and is not designed to offer an unprejudiced accounting of one's payments versus the return in benefits they enjoy. It is based on a preconceived bias against those who have achieved a higher level of prosperity. It has also been designed to benefit those top wage earners who have achieved this prosperity by having benchmarks of income used as a checkpoint after which they pay no additional income taxes on their earnings. To be exempt from paying additional SSI withholding merely because one has earned an income exceeding any predetermined dollar amount is faulty and must be addressed. Likewise, to be required to pay little or no tax based on a limited income lacks the equitable participation of all in the society to give equally in proportion to one's income.

The Tax Code of the United States must be changed to reflect fairness in both the collection of and distribution of federal funds from and to the people.

Let's begin with the obvious problems with Title 26. This is the part of the federal code that deals with taxes and is, essentially, the Tax Code. For many years people have complained that it is

50 AVERAGE AMERICAN POLITICS

just too long, cumbersome, and, quite frankly, confusing. Well, even its very size is open for debate and not just by the average American in this country, but by the very people who have brought this monstrosity to the people, our elected representatives from Congress to the White House.

Here's just a brief list of statements from some of our paid elected officials on the size of this beast:

US Representative John Hostettler (R-IN): "… the Internal Revenue Code and regulations add up to one million words and is nearly seven times the length of the Bible."

US Representative Rob Portman (R-OH): "The income tax code and its associated regulations contain almost 5.6 million words—seven times as many words as the Bible. Taxpayers now spend about 5.4 billion hours a year trying to comply with 2,500 pages of tax laws."

US Representative J.C. Watts, Jr. (R-OK): "The heart of IRS abuse lies in the existing tax code. Most of the folks who work for the IRS are good people just trying to do their job, but they are caught in a bad, overextended tax system. At 3,458 pages, twice the length of the Bible, it's impossible for the average taxpayer to know, understand, and accurately apply its provisions. The length is twice that of the Bible! Even tax experts cannot do so reliably."

US Representative Spencer Bachus (R-AL): "With its 6,000 pages and 500 million words, the complexity of our tax code is the prime source of frustration and anger felt by millions of Americans toward their government."

US Representative Bill Archer (R-TX): "The Internal Revenue Code and regulations now come in at one million words and 9,000 pages."

US Representative Jo Ann Emerson (R-MO): "The Bible, the guide of our lives, is 1,291 pages and contains 774,746 words. But the Tax Code and its regulations, which are referred to by some as a person's worst nightmare come true, are 9,471 pages and over 7 million words."

US Representative Vito Fossella (R-NY): "… the tax code runs 17,000 pages and contains a mind-boggling 5.5 million words. By way of comparison, *War and Peace* is only 1,444 pages and the Bible checks in at 1,291 pages."

US Representative Jim DeMint (R-SC): "The federal tax code with its 44,000 pages, 5.5 million words, and 721 different forms is a patchwork maze of complexity and a testament to confusion over common sense."

US Representative Walter Jones (R-NC): "The IRS tax code is 44,000 pages and growing."

US Representative Bobby Jindal (R-LA): "The current tax code is almost 60,000 pages, longer than the Bible."

US Representative Dave Hobson (R-OH): "… the current tax code . . . at 1.3 million pages is twice the length of Tolstoy's *War and Peace*."

US Representative Nick Smith (R-MI): "… the federal tax code has about four times as many words as the Bible. Accompanying the law are a staggering two-and-a-half-million pages of regulations."

President George W. Bush (R): "The tax code is a complicated mess. You realize, it's a million pages long."

Now, considering the disagreement on how big the document is right now, why should we ever expect these fine upstanding citizen legislators to get together on a fix of this thing?

Surprised? Lord, I hope not. Congress can't agree on anything—especially when it comes to taxes. The camps appear clear from the outside if you listen to the simplistic rants from either side of the aisle. Actually it's the same argument from both sides just with different players involved. First let's look at the arguments for the Tax Code staying the way it is from both sides.

The liberals' argument against touching the Tax Code: "Republicans just want to give tax cuts to the rich so they will continue to vote and finance Republicans running for office. It's all a big kickback." Are they right? Well, in a sense, *yes*.

The conservative argument against touching the Tax Code: "Democrats just want to take money from hardworking middle-class Americans who have earned the money they have and hand it over to those people who either do not or will not work to endear Democratic votes." Are they right? Well, in a sense, *yes*.

Simplistic answers for the easily lead. I was once told that writing a book at the level of a third grader would be the best way to sell it, just like the newspapers. Unfortunately, I can't stand the thought of the only people buying this book being those in the bottom 10 percent of the nation's high school dropouts. So we are going to go just a little deeper into the Tax Code and try to make sense of not just the arguments of the two major political parties, but also look at a way to make the system both fair and friendly for the American people and the American government. If you really aren't interested in knowing how badly you are being raped financially by your government, please go on to the next chapter. But if you think that you are among the lucky ones compared to what awaits your children and the near 80 percent tax load they will carry, then you might want to stick with this chapter for a while. At least until you understand it, even if that means reading it over and over again.

Let's get started....

First, the arguments in their extended form have to really be questioned. The idea that "Republicans just want to give tax cuts to the rich so they will continue to vote and finance Republicans running for office. It's all a big kickback" is, for lack of a better word, correct. But there is much more to the equation than this. Republicans do indeed tend to vote for things that on the surface and to a person who does little more than listen to Liberal talking heads appear to be oriented toward making life better for those who already have a good life or, better yet, The Good Life. According to those same people, the last tax cut that President Bush signed into law rewarded (and I use the word *rewarded* for a reason; it is the way those on the Left like to describe these tax cuts when applied to the rich) those in the top 1 percent of all income earners in the United States. They are the kings of creating a simplistic picture for people to look at so that they can invoke emotion over critical thought. Al Gore's most recent book describes how the brain works when it comes to reading versus seeing pictures through entertainment products.

According to the scientists who sit in Al Gore's Ivory Tower with him, which I believe is located somewhere near Never-Never Land, the brain reacts differently to stimuli according to the way the stimuli get inside. Those watching television and movies are reacting on an emotional level. The brain can tell the difference between real and make-believe just fine; on an intellectual level you know that the child dying on-screen is a highly paid actor who is playing a role scripted by a person who used their imagination to create a fictional world for the watcher to immerse themselves in for a time while escaping from their own reality. All well and good. But at the same time, ever cry at the end of a movie? I'll bet you have but it wasn't because you believed that what had happened was real, it was because your emotions were overloaded with picture and sound and although you knew it was not real, you reacted to it on an emotional level. This is something that liberals have practiced for decades whether they knew what they were doing or not.

On the other hand, people who gain their entertainment through reading are rarely taken in by the emotion of what they are reading because reading is done by a different part of the brain and whatever pictures they might see in their head are being produced by the brain itself and lack the external visual and audible preplanned experience. Your brain still knows that a make-believe situation is at hand, but it is coming to you through only one sense and not a bombardment of sight and sound that trigger an emotional response on multiple planes of your mind's process. (The theater of the mind need not be a dimly lit place.)

The tax cuts were just the latest in a long history of visually aided politicking. This time they used the Lexus as the image of wealth, bad news for Mercedes, Caddy, and BMW. In a number of speeches, sound bites, and news clips the tax cuts were broken down as follows: The top 1 percent of income earners get a tax cut equivalent to the purchase price of a Lexus while working (and notice that word, *working*, as if the rich do not work for what they have) people of the country will see a cut equal to the purchase price of that car's muffler. This is class envy punctuated with images of the rich actually using their savings to go buy a Lexus while the "working-class" folks are out buying mufflers. Ridiculous as it sounds, it worked on many people in this country.

The liberals in this country have had it in for the "rich" for decades, despite the fact that in many cases they are the very "rich" they target. Think about the people you see attacking the rich on a weekly basis. Ted Kennedy, Hillary Clinton, John Edwards, Al Gore, and others are the first to shoot at the rich in this country and what is most interesting is that not one of them has ever created a single thing for the benefit of mankind. Not one of these people listed have owned a business that employed hundreds or thousands of people or added to the economy of more than themselves and those directly around them, and none of them have done it on their own. Kennedy, Now deceased, was the inheritor of the Kennedy fortune created by his father and grandfather; Hillary is the ultimate in coattail riders, gaining her notoriety through her husband. John Edwards made his money the old-fashioned way by suing companies, and Al Gore went, well, from old money to scare money. His fortune was made by his father and the money he has made in recent years has been from his speaking engagements designed to scare people into preparing for the impending end of the planet. Not a single product that has employed "working-class" people, not a single service that benefited more than themselves. But it is those rich people like CEOs of major corporations (*that have buoyed this country through good times and bad, GE, General Motors, IBM, and others*) who are destroying this country with greed in their eyes?

Returning to Lexus cars and their mufflers, liberals love to color a picture of those who have it bad and those who have nothing as somehow virtuous. They believe that all of those people who have money most certainly took it from those who have nothing. This is the fictional stagnant economy picture they like to paint, the "size of the pie never changes" idea. It is like saying that there is only $100 in the entire economy and that is all there is ever going to be; the rich have $80 and the rest of us fight over the remaining $20. Every time the rich make another dollar they take it from the $20, leaving us with $19 to fight over, then $18, $17, and so on. It is a crazy theory that flies in the face of history. Why is this country worth trillions of dollars? Has it always been worth that much? Of course it hasn't; once it was worth nothing but the tobacco and tea we sent to England, beyond that it was not worth a dime.

But they like to push this idea on people who don't take the time to look at things. We are all busy with our lives, our jobs, our kids, our spouses, etc., and often don't take the time to even look at a news story online where we can find additional information. Instead we accept that which is intravenously fed to us from the media and our politicians. But I understand; being an average American I know that people look into those things that matter most to them or that spark some minor interest that needs to be fed. It is part of the reason this book was written. If there is a spark of interest in a reader's mind and he or she goes to the Internet and starts looking around at all the information that is available on any given subject he or she will expand their mind just a bit, then perhaps they will tell another and another. Soon you have a truly informed population and, more importantly, an informed electorate.

As you research these things you find that more often than not there lies within all of it a grain of truth, so long as your view of the subject does not change. The idea that Republicans just protect the rich is an idea that if you want to prove it going in you surely will. Tax cuts that are based on a percentage reduction of what you already pay will always benefit the producers of great wealth with a bigger cut in dollars than the poor and middle class for one basic reason: They pay a hell of a lot more than you and I do. If you are paying $100,000 in taxes based on a 30 percent tax rate and the government comes along and cuts your tax rate to 15 percent you will see a $50,000 decline in what you have to pay, thus giving you $50,000 more to spend, invest, or to use as you see fit.

By the same token, if you pay $4,000 in taxes based on a 10 percent income tax rate and the government comes along with that very same 50 percent cut in your tax rate, making it 5 percent, you will see the same 50 percent savings the rich person saw—an increase of $2,000 more in your pocket.

So you start thinking, "They still get a lot more money than I get" and you start to feel bad. Go get a better job! Don't sit there and start thinking they are getting something you are not getting and life isn't fair. Do something about it. Get more education, work more than one job, help your spouse get a better job; don't sit there thinking you got screwed. You are the sum total of your experiences up to the age of eighteen, beyond that you have the control to remake your life any way you want. They have what they have in most cases because they busted their butts to get it. Class envy is the most effective weapon the liberals have. The idea that others are out there living the so-called Good Life with money they had handed to them down through the generations is, for the most part, bunk. There really isn't that much old money in this country. Most millionaires in this country are self-made and most did it through real estate. Don't sit there and wish for someone else's life because you get their problems, too. Like when a Democratic Congress and president come along and decide that you need to pay more in taxes because you have more than the other guy. Let's say you have this $100,000 income tax bill and the guy a mile away has a bill of $4,000 per year. The government lays a tax increase at the feet of everyone in the country (despite what the Democrats say, they raise taxes on everyone when they do it, everyone, that is, except one class of people, those who pay no taxes at all, but we will talk about that in a minute) but when they do it they do it this way: You get an increase from, say, 30 percent to 45 percent while the guy down the street sees his go from 10 percent to 12 percent. You have just been handed a 50 percent increase in your tax burden while the guy with less money has been handed a 20 percent increase. Your tax bill just went into the stratosphere, $150,000, while the other guy's has just gone up to $4,800. Now what is fair about that? Both of you rely on the same military to defend you, you rely on the same federal highways to get you around, you both rely on the same EPA, Homeland Security, the same FDA, FAA, and every other federal agency or administration out there. So why should you pay more than a person who has less to offer? Because we are a society that works as a whole, not as little individuals who can pick and choose where they want their money to go.

However, you should not have to carry a burden disproportionate to the burden someone else carries, should you? The idea of shared sacrifice is a good one to look at right about now.

There's an old joke about a reporter who finally gets the interview of a lifetime. He gets to interview God face-to-face, mano a mano, Barbara Walters or Larry King style. So he starts with a simple question about time, something only God can truly understand. He asks God, "Lord, how long is a million years to you?" God replies, "About a minute." The reporter then asks, "Lord, how much is a million dollars to you?" God replies, "About a penny." The reporter then gets up the courage to ask God, "Lord, can I have a penny?" to which a loving and caring God replies, "Sure, give me a minute and I'll get that for you."

When we are talking about taxes we need to look at it not in dollars and cents but in shared sacrifice. Do you think the tax increase on a so-called rich person is harder or easier than on a middle-class person? You can't really answer that unless you know how much the increase is. When our government does an increase they do it in steps or tiers. And when they do a tax cut they tend to do it in these same tiers. The poor pay nothing in income tax because we have a magic number you have to hit before you are taxed to try to give those who are really strapped some help by not taking yet more money from them. The middle class, union laborer, police officer, factory worker, teacher, salesman, etc., are given a tax cut or increase that generally will not add too much of a benefit or burden to them as they are seen rightfully as the "backbone of America." The rich, however, are not viewed in this same saintly way. An increase on them is much higher than for anyone else. And this is what the Democrats call "Paying Their Fair Share." But there isn't anything fair about it.

An increase of zero percent on one part of the population, followed by an increase of 10 to 20 percent on another part of the population, followed by an increase of 35 to 50 percent on yet another part is just plain ole class warfare. This is the label the Left loves to throw at Republicans as they cut taxes. Again, no cut for the poor because they don't pay any, followed by a 10 to 20 percent for the middle class, followed by a "huge" tax cut of 35 to 50 percent on the "dirty rich."

They're both right. It is idiocy at its finest and brings us back around to the conservative argument about Democrats and their tax policies. "Democrats just want to take money from the hardworking middle-class and successful Americans who have earned the money they have and hand it over to those people who either do not or will not work" (and here's the clincher) "so they will continue to vote Democrat."

Is it true? *Yes.* To a point.

Both Democrats and Republicans have two jobs when they get into Congress or the White House. We like to think that their first order of business is to do the peoples' business. But oftentimes it is the second more personal job that dominates much of their time and energy: getting reelected. This means fund-raising.

So, you might ask, "Why is it that in this country there are poor and there are rich anyway? Don't we all have the same opportunity?" Why, yes, we do. We all have equality of opportunity to succeed in America, regardless of color, race, sex, etc. What we don't have is equality of talent, timing, and determination. I like to call it TTD. You can call it what you like but any way you slice it it's the truth.

Let's look at each one as it pertains to equality in America.

## *Talent*

Not everyone is going to be able to catch on to the concept of the next big thing. Bill Gates and a few others understood at the time what personal computers would mean to our lives. They also had a knack for understanding how a computer would do what it does. This is God-given talent. You can learn anything you want in life, but generally you will learn more about something that interests you than something that does not. I can tell you that if I had been an adult in the 1970s I would have missed the boat on computers just like most of you did or would have. Why? I have little interest in the subject. The only reason I am using one right now is that I view it as a tool to do a job, the job I am performing right now. Beyond that, I am not that interested in the conceptual stuff, the ins and outs of what makes it work, or the potential it has to do other stuff in my life. I'm sure this thing can do a bunch more than I require of it but I just don't care that much so long as I can look up information online, read the news, watch a funny video once in a while, and write this book. To put it plainly, I have no talent for this stuff because I have limited interest in it.

## *Timing*

This one is more open to the masses; however, it's not a question of how, but of when; not of what you know but when you know it. Think again of our example of Bill Gates. If he had been born just fifty years earlier we might still be waiting for someone to really see the potential of computers in everyday life. Fifty years later and he might have missed his calling. Henry Ford did similar great works with assembly lines. He didn't invent them, nor did Gates invent the computer, but they were there at a time when the potential was ripe for the picking, and they had the talent to see the potential in the idea. Gutenberg did the same with the printing press. He saw that it was a tool for getting the Bible out to more people. Look at Van Braun with rockets and Art Linkletter with the hula hoop, people who were there at the right time when the right idea was launched. Like you've heard before, sometimes timing is everything.

## Determination

But even if you have the talent to do something big and the timing is right there is still one thing that you have to possess to put the whole thing in motion. Without this one simple thing the talent will die on the vine and time will run out. You have to have the determination to see it through. We might well still be building cars one at a time and I might have been typing this book on an IBM roller ball typewriter if Henry Ford had not actively gone after the financing to build his first plant and Bill Gates had not started Microsoft in his garage on a shoestring budget. (Sidebar: It was Harvey Firestone who helped get Ford going because he could produce tires for Henry's cars and it was Xerox who got Gates going because of his lesser-known but nearly just as indispensable invention, the computer mouse.) There are more people in this country today who are new millionaires than those who inherited the money. Think about that for a moment. There is one young, Black American who grew up dirt-poor, Farrah Gray, who started out mixing hand lotions to produce a new lotion that he then started selling in little bottles under his own brand name. A few years later the kid was taking care of his entire family and making over a million dollars per year and he did it all by the age of fourteen. If you want to see a truly inspirational story, you should Google Farrah Gray and read his story.

Had any of these people not attempted to follow through on their dreams, they would have stayed just that, dreams. Mark Victor Hansen, co-author of the *Chicken Soup for the Soul* series of books, tells the story at his seminars of having gone to sixty-plus publishing companies with the ideas for his books. In every instance he was handed rejection. Imagine rejection, rejection, rejection on a monumental scale. Ross Perot, the genius behind Texas Instruments was shot down a similar number of times. Both men shared the determination to go into one more company, one more publisher, and ask again. In the process the idea stayed the same, the timing was still ripe, but the determination to succeed undoubtedly caused a focusing of the message, a pattern of what almost opened doors and what turned customers or potential business partners off. It was, in fact, the rejection that made the process better for both, or at least their ability to convey the idea clearer.

Probably the best example of this was told by Paul Harvey, the man who brought us *The Rest of the Story* on radio for decades. Paul tells the story of a couple of friends, one a successful businessman and the other a dreamer who had failed at nearly every business he had come up with. There names were Walter and Art.

As the story goes, Walter had an idea and really wanted Art to benefit from it. The only problem with it was Walter's track record. Walter was the one with the piss-poor record on making his dreams come true. So he approaches Art and asks him to go for a drive through some farm country. As they go through the miles of orchards, Walter starts telling Art about his idea, something that had never been attempted before. Art listens intently as Walter spins his web with excitement, but, alas, Art has to tell Walter that with his track record, he just couldn't see the vision working out. Not to be deterred, Walter finds other folks who can see and feel the potential and goes ahead with his plans.

Art Linkletter was there on the opening day of Disneyland. And for his honest friendship and because Art was still a businessman who could now see the potential (he just needed a little visual aid, like Cinderella's castle in full-size, to make the point) he is asked if he would still like to participate in Walt Disney's dream. Art accepts and asks for just one thing, the rights to sell cameras and film as the sole distributor inside Disneyland for the next several years. Talk about Timing, Talent, and Determination and a win-win situation for all of us. Art passed earlier this year but thankfully this story was shared and hopefully will inspire many more such stories.

So you can see where TTD comes into play and why it is often the only thing that stands between those who have "made it" and those who have not. But make no mistake; TTD is a factor in everything from education to social work. If you don't believe me, just look at your children's or grandchildren's report cards the next time they come in. You will see that the subjects your kids enjoy, have an interest in, or are taught by a charismatic teacher are the subjects they do best in. I am a perfect example of this, having received great grades in science, government, and agriculture classes while struggling with math and English. The only English class I ever really enjoyed was one semester of creative writing, and while I enjoyed the process of placing your ideas on paper, I still got less than admirable grades in it because of the technicalities of the English language. There are just too many rules for my lack of talent to learn it. Yet here is the culmination of that determination to write a book. Just because you lack one of the three, or even two of the three, does not mean you give up on your dream. You make a choice to succeed or not to succeed based on your actions. And whichever one you choose is exactly what you will get.

When applied to social work it is most clearly seen by churches like the Catholic Church (of which I am not a member). Catholic Social Services helps millions all over the world. If we apply the TTD theory to them it becomes crystal clear as to why. First, because they do not manufacture anything that might pull resources from their many projects, they have time to work at it. But more importantly, you have to recall that the Church came to power during one of the darkest times in human history, the Dark Ages, so their *timing* was perfect to start focusing on a singular objective. Clergy members are people who have made a choice based on a belief that this is their calling in life and have an interest in serving humanity, giving them the basis for the *talent* they bring to the table. Finally, few can argue that the Catholic Church lacks *determination* when they believe they are charged by God with assisting humanity the world over.

Unfortunately, it is this same TTD that the US Government applies to the Tax Code in this country. Our elected officials have only one job to do: ensure that those programs they create are funded. Although many would argue that what they might have in the timing and determination departments, they lack in the talent department. This might explain why the Tax Code is a fluid and constantly changing menagerie of nearly unlimited laws. It might also explain why most government programs have simply not created the outcomes for which they were created. Look at the Great Society and the end of poverty, Social Security and the end of elderly poverty, or the Department of Energy (or any of the lesser-known but just as aggressively lobbied for programs that individual members of Congress, presidents, and groups of government entities continue to fund with your money through our wonderful system of taking from people who work hard and giving to those who will not, cannot, or simply do not work).

Our tax system is convoluted to say the least. It makes no sense and is an embarrassment to our otherwise great country. Punishing achievement while rewarding failure was not what the Founding Fathers had in mind. They saw a people who would take care of one another in times of tragedy, provide for those who truly could not provide for themselves, and a people who would grow through success after success into something wonderful based on the freedom to achieve.

But what kind of tax system would work? A simple one, for starters, that applies the code evenly to all participants. As the system sits right now we give passes to nearly 50 percent of the country on paying income taxes, we provide too much corporate welfare to companies, and we take too large a portion from those who create jobs, thus stifling our economic growth as a whole. There are a number of tax systems that could be employed, from the flat tax where every citizen regardless of income pays the same percentage of their income to the federal government to usage taxes that are based on how much you buy or use each year, almost like a national sales tax. The point is that these need to be explored more. But any change has to be applied fairly and evenly across the board to all taxpayers. In making the changes necessary we need to calculate honestly the income the government needs to perform its job. But its job also needs to be redefined. People tell us that in order to cover all the necessary tax revenues the government needs (and this includes state, federal, county, city, and other localities) we would have to use a flat tax of at least 23.5 percent. But here again we have the states funneling the taxes to the federal government. Then they sit around and wait for the block grants to do what they will with their share and still have the federal government's restrictions on what money can be used for what projects. For more on how the proposed flat tax might work, look it up at http://www.fairtax. org/site/PageServer?pagename=about_faq_answers.

But here is another idea whose time may have come: STOP MAKING IT COMLICATED!!! As you go to that site, look at all the talk of rebates per month funded with your tax dollars for essential items like food, clothing, and shelter. One fact they do point out is that corporations pay no tax. Oh, they do, but they get that money from you in the form of higher costs for the goods and services you buy.

I need to stress this one more time: The flat tax as proposed is to replace the current system, not reform it. It is also designed to ensure the same revenue comes into Washington as the old system provided. That is a major problem for me as the government is too involved with too many things as it is. This is why I say we need to redefine government's role in our lives first and reduce what it needs to perform its new (actually its original) more limited job description. Then remake the tax system in that image. Perhaps only a 15 percent flat tax would work then. Why change to a system that takes just as much money from you as the old one just because it is easier to calculate?

Usage taxes work in much the same way. It would again be set up to provide the same revenue that the federal government and state government currently collect. But that is not the idea behind changing the government's role in our lives.

As I mentioned in the first chapter, we will need far less revenue for the government once we get them back in their box and doing what they were intended to do.

# Chapter 5

The US Military is not a subject for social engineering, nor are our senior citizens. Healthcare is not something the government should have any further involvement in, especially considering the poor job they have done in the running of that portion of healthcare they took over decades ago.

Our military is an all volunteer force composed of members from all social and economic backgrounds. It is a force inseparable from the common stock from which our country is woven and as such should not be used for the purpose of contrived or spurious experimentation.

## The US Military Is Not a Place for Social Engineering

For the last twenty years the military of the United States has been a breeding ground for social experimentation. From women in foxholes to gays openly serving, it has seen the stuff that people would have cringed about fifty years ago and thought to themselves there is simply no way it will ever happen. Yet from the election of 1992 to today, the military has been seen as the federal government's personal laboratory for all things experimental when it comes to the social changes it wants to see in American life.

In January of 1993, as President Clinton was ushered into office, a Hollywood liberal well known for his beliefs was standing in the crowd. That man was actor Ron Silver. Best known recently for his stint on *The West Wing* playing Bruno Gianelli, an advisor to the character President Bartlett played by Martin Sheen (a major Hollywood liberal), he had come a long way in his beliefs since that time. But on that day he still had a liberal streak and when someone complained about a flyover of military aircraft he reminded them, "those are our planes now." This is the mentality of many people on the Left. It is a "them versus us" mentality that no president can change, not even the Great Evolver, President Obama.

President Clinton was not even in office yet, having just been elected, when on Veteran's Day 1992 he announced that he would be lifting the ban on gays in the military. The idea that gay soldiers should be allowed to openly serve in the military is absurd. Yet once the liberals had a toehold in the door they made the jump from gays openly serving directly to equality for women in combat situations.

Contrary to popular belief, there are fundamental differences between men and women physically. I know this might be hard for some of you to understand, but traditionally men have 20 to 30 percent greater upper body strength than women. This comes in handy when pulling a two-hundred-pound man out of the way of oncoming fire or lugging sixty pounds of supplies up a hill, in addition to the eight-pound gun that you are shooting that gives off ten pounds of recoil pressure with each shot. In addition, men have a 25 to 30 percent greater aerobic capability, which comes into play when running with the same supplies, guns, and ammo.

This is not to say that women cannot play a major role in the military. Women have for the entire history of this country played important supporting roles to the men serving in the military. But when it comes to combat situations on the ground, they simply do not have, in most cases, the physical aptitude to perform at the same levels as men.

Some of you will argue that if a woman passes the tests at the same level as a man what's the issue? Well if that were the case I would have to agree with you. But what happened was women were not exactly performing at the same level as men. Instead there has been a normalization of the tests. The passing A grade for women training is equivalent to the D grade of the men, yet they claim these to be equal. Put plainly, a women performing physically at 60 percent of a man is not equal to the man's physical ability.

Then there are the very real issues of the psychological effects on the men in those combat conditions where women serve. Most men, and I say this from commonsense experience, will go to great pains to ensure the safety of women over even their own personal safety. One reason is our culture as a whole. We are raised knowing you don't hit women; we are raised knowing that women are the "fairer" sex and that men are supposed to look out for their safety. Men serving with men also tend to build a very real bond of trust as each is sure that the other has the physical capability to intervene on the other's behalf if things get out of hand.

My wife is 5'1" and her weight is proportional to her height (yes, I am a smart married man for not giving her actual weight even though it is nothing for her to be ashamed of, she is a beautiful woman) and I am 6'3" tall and weight in the three-hundred-pound range. As much as I know that my wife would lay her life on the line for me, I would not want her in a foxhole with me. She would be a vicious warrior but despite her desire to come and get me if I was wounded I would still want a guy like my best friend from high school who is 6'1" and weighs two-fifty. He could get me out of wherever I was. This applies to men in the trenches, too.

You see, one of the real threats here is that the military is duty sworn to do what it is told, without the asking of questions. That is a major issue for the men and women who put their lives in harm's way if the people setting the policies regarding them are not taking their actual missions into account. But where that does not apply is in the real world. If a firefighter is forced to be accompanied by a person who has not passed all the tests to ensure an adequate physical ability equal to his own, what are the chances of him taking additional risk to his own life and limb to save someone if he is worried about his partner's ability to come to his rescue should he need help? It sounds like two different subjects, but truth be known, depending on the outcome of how things work in government entities, it oftentimes becomes the policy of the public at large and is applied to all government entities because of the politically correct society in which we now find ourselves.

There are many jobs that men and women do equally well in every respect, and there are many at which women do a much better job; likewise, it must be admitted that there are many jobs men are simply better able to perform than women. This is not sexist in the least; on the contrary, it is simply true. Truth does have a way of being labeled at times with all kind of additional names, many earned but many not.

I do not agree with the argument that women, because of their monthly cycle, are ill suited to serve in the trenches. If that were the case they would be deemed ill suited for all manner of jobs based on that alone. This, of course, is absurd. But admitting the physical difference between the sexes is in no way belittling to either. Those who bring that charge are generally upset with the deal handed to them by nature.

But to the greater degree that what happens in the military and other government agencies influences the country as a whole, we must be wary of any ideas thrown around in government. I know a lot of people don't care for politics and I can understand why, having been involved in studying it for decades, but when you consider that the changes in policy in government affects you in so many ways, it is really in your best interest to pick up at least a passing interest in the process, if not for the outcome of a particular debate, at least for the knowledge of how to arrange your finances to ensure the lowest possible signature on the government's radar.

The government is today using this same technique to affect another major portion of the US economy and that of course is healthcare. I am not willing to speculate on whether or not healthcare reform is going to pass and be taken over by the government, but I will tell you what I hear in the winds. The election of Scott Brown in Massachusetts drastically changed the configuration of the Senate, stealing away from the Democrats that vital 60–40 supermajority. President Obama seems to be unsure what to do with his idea at this point and is actually paying lip service (which must just be killing the likes of Nancy Pelosi and Harry Reid) to the GOP in both houses as he berates them for not jumping in on the fun and passively supporting a bad idea.

Now, whether or not the Obama healthcare initiatives make their way through Congress and come out the other side resembling anything close to the original intent of the president really isn't the issue. The issue is: What are we doing?

Over the last seventy years, we have watched the morphing of Social Security into a creature that cannot be stopped. Social Security is the grandfather of all entitlements. From it sprung the largest of the entitlements we are now forced to maintain. And from this marriage we may be looking at universal healthcare as the legitimate continuation of one bad idea after another. Healthcare represents 16 percent of the US economy, and your government believes that through its participation it will be able to reduce the costs associated with premiums, reduce the overall costs of doctor visits and tests, and reduce the cost of medication, merely through their excellent management techniques. Please excuse me for a moment while I throw up. I again challenge any of you to find the one government program or entitlement that has ever stayed on budget, solved the issue it was intended to solve, and was ended in the time frame originally intended. Don't knock yourself out; you will not find one. You will find a few that were canceled but even those reappear in the record later as some other program that is still with us today. Tracking down programs becomes something like dinosaur hunting. Just when you think something has disappeared from the fossil record, it turns back up, slightly different, but definitely of the same family. This is the case with the push for universal healthcare, single-payer healthcare, or the more commonly referred to Obama Care. Hillary Clinton, during her husband's administration, was not the first to attempt a wholesale governmental takeover of healthcare. It has been alive since the first words of the Social Security program were inked onto paper. Franklin Roosevelt tried it, Truman tried it, Lyndon Johnson tried it, and Carter tried it. And if Obama fails to do it the next Democrat in office will try it. This is the very definition of incrementalism: the step-by-step approach to getting what you want. The amazing thing is the tenacity with which it has been pursued over the last seventy-plus years. Generation after generation of liberal administrations have tackled this issue in some way or another but the ultimate prize, the big payoff so to speak, is the complete takeover by government of the healthcare industry.

Starting in the late 1930s and early 1940s, as the largest expansion of government was under way by the Roosevelt administration (that would be Franklin Roosevelt not Theodore), liberal-minded folks placed a premium on control of public healthcare. If you ask yourself why, you are asking the right question. But the answer, although simple, is also scary. Again it comes back to control. Those who control your access to medical care also control, to a large degree, your life. And if they have control of your life to any degree, which way are you more likely to vote? Well, the theory is that you will vote for those who promise to deliver the most to you through those avenues that they control and that you rely on. This was discovered (actually it's been known since Roman times) by our good liberal friends in the immediate aftermath of the Civil War. As the war came to an end the American Black population was given the right to vote and since the man who saved the union was Abraham Lincoln, a Republican (the first real Republican in the minds of many), they exercised their support for the Republican Party at the ballot box to the tune of 80 to 90 percent. You see, they had been provided with the "most" by the party that held the control over them. Well, with their freedom, which was given through the Republican leadership through the war, they were now free and could now choose what they wanted to pursue, and they did. But in the aftermath of the war, many deals were made in Congress, including a few that would drastically injure the American Black for at least 150 years. One of these deals was one in which the North returned basically complete control over their local governments to the South. While it would be expected that with hostilities ending, the South would be given just that, it was too much control too soon. Those who had lost the war were none too happy about the results. So with the North no longer breathing down their throats about how they treated American Blacks and other minorities they went back to treating them poorly.

Then in the early 1900s there were people who started to feel badly about the way they had treated these people. Deciding that there was an incredible economic opportunity that was being missed, legislation was passed to try to improve the plight of American Blacks in the South. Well, law or no law, the Democrats who had slowly regained a foothold through rigged voting, blocking Blacks from voting, and basically running the South as it had always been run, save for the actual slavery, were not about to go along with these laws.

Enter the 1930s and Franklin Delano Roosevelt. Now here was a man of vision. He saw the need and set out to provide for that need. Understand what I said there—not solve that need, but provide for it. Oh, yes, Roosevelt had stumbled on to something incredible. The ability to gain and maintain a solid voter block based on providing them (the poor) with what they needed through government. Sad as it is, it really was brilliant and completely the opposite of what was good for the people who would be affected by it.

Roosevelt identified two primary groups that would be targeted. First was the elderly, those looking toward retirement.

Although a few different plans had been run up the flagpole in the past, none of them had the sweeping impact the Social Security system would on the mentality of elderly people in this country some forty years later. Voting during this time was mostly done by affluent American Whites. But with the stock market crash of 1929 many of them were no longer as affluent as they had been or wanted to be. This made the idea of a "safety net" rather interesting to them. It was sold as a system that would "supplement" the elderly in their golden years, but what most Americans heard was "retirement" and dropped the supplement part. Because of this I fully believe that many did not save at the rates they would have and as such were forced to have to live on the very system that was meant to merely supplement their own savings. Years later this situation would be the weapon of choice the Democrats would employ election cycle after election cycle; that Republicans were going to take away the elderly folk's Social Security checks. This is something that was never envisioned by any Republican running for office. As we discussed earlier, the idea of privatizing Social Security is only proposed with the assumption that those on it will not lose a dime and those still in line for it will absolutely benefit to the degree to which they qualify.

With the elderly block locked in, the other group was the veterans from the First World War. They were out of work, mad as hell, and looking for an early payout on pensions promised to them by former administrations. Roosevelt solved this with his public works projects, which put millions to work around the country building roads, dams, bridges, and all manner of public projects. However, truth be told, many of these were President Hoover's ideas and the Democratic Congress at the time sat on the legislation. The government spent and spent and spent. It kept the men busy and when the time arrived for elections, they were two blocks that could be counted on to vote for the folks promising to deliver the most through the avenues they controlled. It worked like a charm.

Fast-forward to Medicare, the natural expansion of this project that cemented the elderly as a voting block and made those in their forties and fifties start looking to the benefits they would soon be eligible for. And like magic, another large block was at least partially secured for the Democratic Party.

Now this went along pretty good for a while. The 1950s boomed and people were secure for the most part. The only region of the country that really wasn't swept up with the rising tide was poor American Blacks. Eisenhower was less interested in what was going on here at home with race because he had his eyes overseas where the real issues that could end America were poised (at least we thought so at the time) to pounce at the first sign of weakness. The Soviet Union took up a lot of Eisenhower's time and energy as they would for the next few presidents.

It was Lyndon Johnson who would lock the next group of voters into the Democratic ranks. The Great Society was envisioned as putting an end to the division between the majority White and minority Black in this country. It was sold as a tool for leveling the country out. Too many had been left behind in the economic boom that was America in the 1950s. But what Johnson forgot was that the boom was brought on not by government, but by the people. Government-sponsored segregation was ending and American Blacks were about to be thrust onto the national stage as entrepreneurs with the freedom to vote openly for their best interests. Or perhaps Johnson did see this and figured it was time to strike while the iron was hottest. Simply by creating another segment of society that would be dependent on the government for their daily bread.

There is an inbred spirit in humans to be the best they can be. In America, because of the freedom people have had, they have achieved greatness like no other place on earth. But nothing can kill that spirit like not needing to work as hard to gain any kind of security. What Johnson managed to do was remove the need to work in order to have a roof over your head and food on your table, regardless of how poor that housing was or how lacking the food was. And contrary to popular belief, it was not just American Blacks who were targeted for this dependency; it was in fact the poor in general.

Although at this time leaders in the American Black community like Dr. Martin Luther King Jr. and others were striving for equality of opportunity, pushing for American Blacks to break that mentality of second-class citizenship and for Whites to accept them as equals, the government was eroding their progress right in front of them. Welfare, the cornerstone of the Great Society, was little more than an upgrade from the plantation, but without the required work, making it not only demoralizing but also comfortable enough not to want to work your way off of it (complaint du jour d'histoire' ... we created a leisure class at the lower end of the bell curve).

The second major impact from Welfare was that the government now took the place of the traditional provider for the family, leading to a lesser need for the father in the home in Black communities. Over the next twenty years this spread like a virus and devastated the American Black community. On top of providing for the family, the government also allowed for women with dependant children to increase their check by adding more children to the Welfare roles. Whatever need existed for the father even being in the home outside of producing another child was gone.

I am not the first to write about this. Many Americans who lived this situation have written about it at length. Among them is Star Parker, a syndicated columnist who wrote the book *Uncle Sam's Plantation*. Her first-person account of life on Welfare is startling and eye-opening. So too is the story of her moving out of the system and later being involved in the writing of the 1996 Welfare Reform legislation that was passed by the Republican Congress and signed into law by President Clinton.

The damage done to the Black community is inexcusable and the lives destroyed by this kind of voter block legislation should haunt the liberal establishment nightly. It is this very treatment of a segment of our American family that hundreds of thousands of Americans died to prevent during the Civil War. Instead of using the political capital to promote real change, the Republican Party of the day dropped the ball, allowing the old Southern

Guard to retake that part of the nation and return it to prewar mentalities and allowing the Democratic Party access to cause these people immense harm. I have a friend who witnessed this transition in St. Augustine Florida's Lincolnville District, which was a thriving community of Black-owned businesses in the 1950s and 1960s, but became a crime-ridden slum by the mid-1970s.

The Republican Party owes the South not because of the Black population there, but because of the American population there. Blacks were not the only demographic harmed by Welfare's demoralization. Many poor, uneducated American Whites were also prey to the destructive dependency associated with Welfare.

Now, a little over a decade since the first rollback of this monstrosity in 1996, a new president has decided to kick the doors off this baby and go for broke.

If we do not draw a line in the sand at this point we are never going to end the spiraling of what is essentially socialism from controlling our government for the next forty years. Just look at the entitlements we have today. Social Security is considered the forth rail of government, a Holy Grail, never to be sought for removal or adaptation from the governmental system. You do not mess with the system, even when it is on the verge of going bankrupt, as it has many times in the last three decades. Each president from Reagan forward has tweaked the system slightly to buy the country time. I have always admired Reagan, but he blew this one big-time. What should have happened was a complete overhaul of the entitlement system. Reagan was on the right track when he cut taxes, but he mistakenly made a deal with the Devil on it. A deal was struck with the Democrat-controlled Congress that they would pass tax cut legislation first, then cut spending. The latter never happened.

It should have been then and there that Social Security was reworked into a private savings system for Americans to control. It still isn't too late; its just going to be a much bigger uphill battle now than it might have been then.

So, now you know where this idea came from. You know how it was incrementally pushed from the changes in the systems originally developed inside government to today where it now affects every one of us, either with the insurance we might get stuck with to the taxes we and our children will pay forever to keep it afloat, not to mention the increases they will pay when we are gone as the system runs over budget year after year.

The government starts with a segment of society it can easily control and tries something new. Over time this has proven to help some, destroy most others, and always cost more than expected, but government is judged on the good intentions of the programs these days, not the results. Healthcare, Welfare, Medicare, Social Security, and the military are all perfect examples of how the government moves slowly but persistently toward ever-increasing control of our lives. Though there have been brief reprieves, they never last quite long enough to build into a movement.

Where is our power to change any of it? The same place it has always been, the ballot box.

# Chapter 6

Illegal immigration should be dealt with at the border first.

Any and all legislation impacting immigration should have at its core the premeditated intention of stopping the overwhelming numbers of illegal immigrants coming into this country. Any and all amnesty provisions should be postponed until the immediate problem has been solved. Mexico's involvement in organizing, assisting, and championing illegal immigration from beyond its border with the United States should be met with the most stern of warnings from the United States, and their involvement in any of these activities should be punished by sanctions and or a total reevaluation of any and all financial aid currently being provided by the United States. Canada, too, must be dealt with sternly as their border with the US is just as bad. This is not a moral issue, nor is it an immigration issue, it is a sovereignty issue.

Illegal immigration is the most important issue of our day, beyond healthcare and beyond tax cuts and beyond terrorism, it is the most glaring example of our government not doing what they are constitutionally mandated to do. Every federal official takes an oath to "defend this country from all threats, both foreign and domestic." They also take an oath to "uphold the Constitution." When it comes to securing our borders they have failed miserably on both accounts.

It is estimated that today, living in this country, are twelve to twenty million illegal immigrants. They are not "temporary workers" or "transient populations" or "undocumented workers"; they are illegally in our country and that makes them "criminals." This is not a Left or Right issue no matter how the media tries to spin these concepts. Americans are losing wages, waiting in hospitals, and paying higher and higher insurance rates for both healthcare and auto insurance because of these criminals.

The 9/11 hijackers entered this country illegally, but not though the Mexican–American border. They came through Canada. The Canadian–American border represents the longest undefended border in the world. The difference between Canada and Mexico is that Canada has a working economy much like the US so their citizens are not making a mass exodus across it into our country.

Mexico represents the primary threat to this country, not in military strength and not in economic power but in shear numbers of people infiltrating our society illegally. The cost associated with this invasion is monumental.

The Center for Immigration Studies (yes, there really is a center set up for the study of illegal immigration) puts the cost of illegal immigration as follows:

> Households headed by illegal aliens imposed more than $26.3 billion in costs on the federal government in 2002 and paid only $16 billion in taxes, creating a net fiscal deficit of almost $10.4 billion, or $2,700 per illegal household.
>
> Among the largest costs are Medicaid ($2.5 billion); treatment for the uninsured ($2.2 billion); food assistance programs such as food stamps, WIC, and free school lunches ($1.9 billion); the federal prison and court systems ($1.6 billion); and federal aid to schools ($1.4 billion).
>
> With nearly two-thirds of illegal aliens lacking a high school degree, the primary reason they create a fiscal deficit is their low education levels and resulting low incomes and tax payments, not their legal status or heavy use of most social services.

On average, the costs that illegal households impose on federal coffers are less than half that of other households, but their tax payments are only one-fourth that of other households.

Many of the costs associated with illegals are due to their American-born children, who are awarded U.S. citizenship at birth. Thus, greater efforts at barring illegals from federal programs will not reduce costs because their citizen children can continue to access them.

If illegal aliens were given amnesty and began to pay taxes and use services like households headed by legal immigrants with the same education levels, the estimated annual net fiscal deficit would increase from $2,700 per household to nearly $7,700, for a total net cost of $29 billion.

Costs increase dramatically because unskilled immigrants with legal status—what most illegal aliens would become—can access government programs, but still tend to make very modest tax payments.

Although legalization would increase average tax payments by 77 percent, average costs would rise by 118 percent.

All in all the total federal cost of illegal immigration is approximately $346 billion. As I said, that is just the federal cost. The state of California reports that it spends over $10 billion annually, Florida reports:
1. $3.4 billion a year to educate illegal immigrant children and the US-born children of illegal immigrants.
2. $290 million a year on unreimbursed healthcare for illegal aliens.
3. $90 million a year to incarcerate criminal illegal aliens.

The total represents an annual cost to each of Florida's native-born-headed households of $678. The worst part for Florida is that this cost has doubled since 2005.

Virginia, not exactly a state that comes to mind when one talks about illegal immigration, reports spending $1.7 billion a year on the problem.

If we laid out all the states we would be looking at another $40 billion. Add that to the federal cost and you come in just shy of $400 billion a year. That is four times the cost of the proposed Obama healthcare plan for a year or equal to the cost of running both fronts in Iraq and Afghanistan in the War on Terror for a year. This is a war, too, and one that we cannot afford to lose.

I lived in Arizona for eight years and the cost of living in a city that is a central hub for illegal immigrant activity is even worse. From Phoenix, Arizona, a network spreads out across the nation transporting illegals to Chicago, Atlanta, Denver, Washington State, and just about every other state that is not right on the border with Mexico. Drop houses are a nightly staple of the local news with anywhere from ten to one hundred illegals found at a pop. They are brought to the states by Coyotes who take their money and bring them as far as Phoenix where others are supposed to pick them up and take them to other locations. But when the heat gets turned up they just leave them there. These people are found in some of the worst shape people can be found in and it is sad. If our country just secured our border they wouldn't end up this way.

How exactly do I propose we secure our borders? Well, legally, first of all. We have in this country a law referred to as the Posse Comitatus Act. The Posse Comitatus Act states: "Whoever, except in cases and under circumstances expressly authorized by the Constitution or Act of Congress, willfully uses any part of the Army or the Air Force as a posse comitatus or otherwise to execute the laws shall be fined under this title or imprisoned not more than two years, or both"(18 U.S.C. §1385). This has been a major stumbling block for years for the idea of sending the military down to the border to defend it. What this says, in essence, is that our military cannot be used to enforce civilian law.

Constitutionally speaking, border issues, the jumping of the border, are covered under civil law. Thus, putting the military on the border cannot be done, right? But the military could be used to repel an invasion from a foreign army. So, the question begs, is it the Mexican Army crossing the border? Well, no, it is not. The next question must be: What is Mexico doing to stop this from happening?

Would you believe absolutely nothing? You got it, not a thing to stop their best and brightest from leaving the country. In fact, they are helping them leave.

Over the past few years the Mexican government has started handing out pamphlets telling people when the best time of year is to brave the deserts of the Southern United States, what supplies they should take (like water, food, blankets, etc.), and even what to say should they encounter the US Border Patrol. These pamphlets even have maps in them so the illegal does not get lost on his quest to break our laws.

While it is nice that they care about their citizens making it across the desert safely, it is reprehensible that they are actually getting assistance from those on the northern side of the border. Who, you ask? Would you believe your current head of Homeland Security, Janet Napolitano? As the former governor of Arizona she was instrumental in approving a plan to build, at American taxpayer expense, several "humanitarian" water stops along the most used routes from northern Mexico to the US. Not those that people drive on, but those most likely to be used by illegals crossing the desert.

I know, it makes you just want to scream. And now she runs Homeland Security. When she was first elected governor of Arizona I had high hopes for her. The state enjoyed a one billion dollar surplus and low taxes. She spoke openly about the border being an issue of importance for Arizonans and the nation as a whole. She placed six thousand National Guard troops down south to try to coax President Bush into doing something concrete about the issue that causes the biggest headache for border states like Arizona, Texas, New Mexico, and California. But then the word got out that the National Guard troops were shuffling paperwork and freeing up the Border Patrol to make more runs down by the actual border itself. Why would she not fully commit these troops to patrolling the border? You guessed it, the Posse Comitatus Act. I could live with that because at least it appeared that she was trying everything within the law to stop the tide of illegal immigrants entering Arizona. At the time I lived in Phoenix, so it was a local issue for me, too.

But then she flipped and started pushing for these watering holes. Then when the chance to return the surplus money to Arizonans came up she instead offered only 10 percent of it to taxpayers and the rest on education and *watering holes*. The result was that she left office for her new gig, leaving a state now hundreds of millions in the red as the economy tanked. And now that Arizona education has that big budget it can't be touched because no politician in Arizona has the guts to get real about it.

Her spending policies aside, however, we were talking about immigration policy. We have watched from the sidelines as southern border state after border state goes broke. Not to blame it all on illegal immigrants, but they certainly haven't helped the situation. We have watched as California has gone essentially broke. Arizona runs a huge deficit now and between the two of them, over 35 percent of the people they incarcerate are "undocumented aliens." These are costs that have to be paid. They should be paid by the one entity that is doing the least to stop the flow of illegals, Uncle Sam. But the federal government is too busy trying to expand healthcare, something that had Rep. Joe Wilson not called President Obama on quite so publically, the illegals may have finally had legal access to as well. It is bad enough that illegal immigrants add daily to the healthcare issues we face in this country, from leaving unpaid bills that we get to cover to the diseases they are not tested for before entering across the deserts.

Those who enter the country legally must pass a health inspection prior to being allowed to enter. Nothing too invasive, just the basics. Do they have a cough, fever, have they been immunized for measles, mumps, rubella—all the things that we require our kids to have before entering school. But some illegals carry with them things far worse. Smallpox has seen a reemergence, as has the various flu mutations that we hear so much about. Without any kind of filter on these people they carry with them the possible means for a pandemic.

I am a big proponent of the globalization of the planet. We do have to work with, trade with, and deal with our neighbors. We all know this, even those who would rather build giant walls and cut us off from the rest of the world; they too know this will never work. We need gates, ways to interact, and ways by which we can protect ourselves when the need arises. Last year the Swine Flu took hold in Mexico and within weeks it had crossed the border. Now nobody can say for sure if it was a legal immigrant, illegal immigrant, or a US citizen returning home who first brought it north, but what can be said is that we have a better chance of finding it if we know where everyone is coming and going through.

Our nation's education has gone in the toilet, as we discussed earlier. Part of that problem can be linked to the increase in illegals entering the country as well as the NEA. When teachers have to teach the subject in two languages, it takes away from the kids in the class who do speak English. California represents the very worst of this, and as a former California student, I can attest to this myself although I lived in a town that was primarily English speaking. I was member of the FFA, the Future Farmers of America, and I participated in something called "Opening and Closing" ceremony competitions around the state. Listening to teenagers attempting to speak from a prearranged speech that everyone had to do that was the same for everyone involved, it was clear that for many of these kids, the English language was relatively new. This is not to belittle their attempts in an organization that has given us presidents, but it is indicative of the issues going on in that particular area of the country and others throughout the nation.

Since the 1960s (when illegal immigration really took hold) the educational level in this country has started to diminish and it is a shame. We are the richest country in the world and we spend more per pupil than any country on earth. I, for one, expect better results. Those are hard to deliver when nearly a fourth of your students are not speaking English as their primary language as is the case in many Southern California school districts.

So, how do we make the borders secure? First of all, we take it seriously and we see the issue clearly. It is not racism that motivates this drive; it is in fact the sovereignty of our country. If we can find $1 trillion to fight a war in Iraq then we can find the money to secure our borders. That has to be the first step. Dealing with those that are already here is secondary. They will assimilate to our culture over time as did the Italians, the Irish, and all the others who came here to be Americans. We also need to stop the hiring of illegals period and introduce some real nationalistic values in the businesses where employment is in question.

We first build the necessary fences to slow the tide. Then we increase Border Patrol surveillance of the areas hardest hit while not forgetting the other areas. This sin of the past has been our policy. We dump men and equipment in a bad area and watch the decline only to see increases in other areas. We also need to open more crossing areas and man them properly and inspect every car, every truck, and every load that crosses them.

The other major part government must play in this, and it will be hard for them to do it unless we have better representation, is laying the rules out for foreign aid to Mexico. They must stop helping their people leave. And if it takes stopping US dollars from crossing the border for a week, a month, or a year to make the point, then we have to do it. Mexico has to take some responsibility in this mess and they have to recognize the huge cost and toll losing people takes on them.

There should not be a single dollar spent in Mexico until they begin enforcement of their northern border. Right now, for those of you unaware, there happens to be a major drug war going on just over our border with Mexico. Drug dealers are shooting people left and right because our good neighbor to the south can't control its own crime problem. Their idea of controlling it is to let us worry about it as it bubbles over into US territory.

Mexico is a sovereign country and they certainly do not allow for the jumping of their borders on their southern end; in fact, there are many stories indicating that they take a rather harsh view of illegals entering their country, up to and including shooting them. That certainly is not what I am proposing here, but they know the devastation an illegal population can produce in their own country yet they dislike our desire to control our border. Actually, they are quite happy with the arrangement as it is now. They get to rid themselves of the unskilled labor they have by exporting them to us and we still go down there and spend a lot of US dollars in their economy. And with NAFTA in effect, we even build them plants to operate and create jobs for their more skilled laborers.

This needs to stop and stop cold in its tracks if we are ever going to gain their assistance in controlling the ever-growing issue of border security.

After we gain control of our border we then need to decide how we want to deal with the ongoing situation of the current population of illegal immigrants in this country. Rounding them all up may be the preferred plan by many, but I believe it is unreasonable to do so, especially when many have been working, paying taxes, and have raised or are raising their kids here, many of whom are citizens by birth.

But this is America and we are a nation of laws. We do not forgive the breaking of laws in this country so there has to be some penalty for having broken the first law when they got here. Perhaps fines, penalties, or denial of actual citizenship while allowing them to stay without access to public entitlement systems for a period of time. We have to punish them somehow. But at the same time they need to understand why.

Their children who were born here, I must agree, have the same right to US citizenship any other native-born American has. But perhaps going forward we need to alter the laws regarding anchor babies born in this country by illegal immigrants. Instant deportation might be one that needs to be looked at seriously. But whatever it is, we need to apply it going forward and not to those already here. That ship has sailed and it is too late to clean that mess up.

We are a country of immigrants and that can never be forgotten, but you must enter legally otherwise you have trespassed on the very Constitution you now wish to be protected by.

There is another aspect of illegal immigration that must be mentioned at this point. This is the aspect of Aztlan, the fictional Chicano country linked with Mexico that is said to lay in the Northern Territory lost to the Americans. This plot of land includes Colorado, California, Arizona, Texas, Utah, New Mexico, Oregon, and parts of Washington. No small parcel of land.

According to California's Santa Barbara school district's Chicano Studies textbook—*The Mexican American Heritage*, by East Los Angeles high school teacher Carlos Jimenez—this land is rightfully Mexico's regardless of a war and a payment of $15,000,000 by the United States to Mexico.

The mouthpiece for this plan is any number of organizations collectively claiming to be La Raza. La Raza is essentially a movement to repatriate those states back to Mexico. Groups like OLA (Organization for the Liberation of Aztlan), The Brown Berets de Aztlan, the "Nation of Aztlan," and La Raza Unida Party are but a few of those pushing for this idea. What better way to repatriate land than to make sure those living on the land to be taken and those who wish to take it all speak the same language? It is the very argument I am making for English alone to be taught in schools unless as an elective in high school or beyond.

The Mexican government does not publically endorse the La Raza movement, but can you imagine the natural resources that would be theirs if they were only partially successful in retaking California alone? Agriculture, oil, port access, and the list continues.

Now, I understand this is a stretch of the imagination for many of you and I feel the same way about it to be honest. However, you cannot ignore an impassioned people hell-bent on taking land. Historically, it is second only to religion for reasons to wage war.

To properly frame the La Raza movement one has to equate their demands to others operating under similar false assumptions of ownership and disenfranchisement. Allow me to introduce you to the Palestinians.

For starters, there is no such thing as Palestine. It was the remnants of the Ottoman Empire, which had collapsed after ruling the area since the 1600s. Modern-day Syria was controlled by the French as was Transjordan, until a switch was made in trade for the Golan Heights region from the British who controlled most of the remaining land. Lots of swapping and trading later, with mandates from the League of Nations (predecessor to the United Nations), the entire area was collectively referred to as Arab Palestine with pockets carved out including Christian and Jewish territories.

At this point is seemed as though a new country might be formed, so the Jewish people took advantage of the lull in fighting and started repatriating to their historic homeland. Within just a few years Jews had built up a solid population, created trade routes, and were for all intents and purposes living in the area and making the area work. Understand this, Israel isn't heaven on earth, it is a dusty, rocky region not that conducive to crops and devoid of most natural resources save those found in dried lakes and seabeds. For a people with no country, knowing this was once their ancestral land, the Jews made every effort to create a community in an attempt to retake the land that had once been theirs by birthright.

During this time, the Arabs were attempting to do the same thing, but with far less impressive results. In 1936, literacy among Jews was reported to be 86 percent and only 22 percent for Arabs in the region. Income-wise, the Jews were fast creating a real economy, grossing an average 2.5 times that of their Arab counterparts. It started to become clear that Arabs were unhappy with the British (heard that before) and led a revolt between 1936 and 1939. It was quelled for a time while a partition agreement was worked out but that failed and fighting resumed, finally ending in late 1939. It was during this time that the Jewish people were targeted more and more because they had supported the British in the fight to contain the Arab uprising.

This pretty much continued all the way through World War II. During this time the Jewish people again sided with the British. The Palestinian Arabs, for the most part, saw the Axis Powers as a way to get rid of the British and the Jews at the same time.

The end of WWII found the British and the Jews on opposite sides of the fence concerning the immigration of Jews to the territory, so the Jews told the British to get out. Not wanting to leave in shame, the British asked the newly formed United Nations to take control of the area (yes, the same UN we see today managing to make a mess of everything they touch). The Brits' story was that they did not want to deal with the area unless Arabs and Jews could get along. (Note to self—look up the last time we tried this and look for different results.) The UN then came up with a plan that the Jews accepted but the Arabs did not. Eventually, as all great nations must have growing pains, a civil war broke out between the Arabs and Jews and the Arabs had defeat handed to them by the Jews.

Finally, a deal was struck and Israel became a state, with the West Bank and Eastern Jerusalem belonging to Jordan and Egypt too over Gaza.

That worked for about a minute. Between Egypt, Israel, and the UN there was a bunch of little agreements dealing with land movement over the next few years. Then in June of 1967 Israel had had enough and took the whole thing over in the Six-Day War. Since then *Palestine* refers to basically any part of Israel the Arabs want to take back.

Since that time it has been a constant thorn in Israel's side with rockets coming in and out of Syria, Jordon, and Egypt. Jordon and Egypt finally signed a peace deal with Israel in the 1970s but Syria and Lebanon have continued to act like spoiled children egged on by Iran.

Now let's apply this same situation to Aztlan. La Raza are the Palestinians. They lost the land in war and land lost in war is rightfully the victor's. But to show we had no hard feelings, we even cut Mexico a check. In essence, we bought the land we had already won in battle, making it doubly ours (sounds childish but it is the only way I can think of explaining how much the United States has rights to that land).

Now, La Raza organizations have yet to launch missiles over the Mexican–American border and they have yet to make a deal with Canada to squeeze us for the land, but the intention to retake it is just as strong in these organizations as that of Arabs inside the Palestinian Liberation Organization (PLO) once headed by Yasser Arafat. And if there is one lesson to be learned from watching Israel it is this: "Victory over an aggressor is not complete until the aggressor gives up the fight." That means one of two things, either the aggressor concedes defeat or he is dead.

La Raza is not Mexico, nor is the PLO Egypt, Syria, or Iran, but both of their funding comes from somewhere. Consider this a cautionary tale.

# Chapter 7

Global warming is a scam perpetrated primarily by the United Nations.

Over the last several years the United Nations and many in the US Government have tried long and hard to make you believe that the end of the world is coming and that it is your fault. They site studies done by the United Nations' Intergovernmental Panel on Climate Change (IPCC) and make claims that mankind is killing the planet because of our cars, our clothes, our cattle, and our very way of life. The industrialization of the planet is causing great billowing clouds of carbon dioxide to lock in the sun's heat and cause a slow but perceptible warming to occur on the planet as measured by very technical instruments around the globe. The polar ice is melting and the polar bear is becoming extinct. Sea levels are rising and many low-lying cities around the world are just years or decades away from being inundated with water. The changing climate is on the verge of causing heat to dry out crops and make planting and harvesting food stocks impossible in many areas of the world, bringing prosperity to other parts of the world where today it is too cold to grow most crops. It will cause regional wars over supplies of water and massive starvation sufficient to wipe out a third of the world's population in the next one to two hundred years.

We must change our habits and lifestyles to stop this catastrophe from coming, but then again it may already be too late. They claim that tornadoes and hurricanes, cyclones, El Niño and La Niña will get stronger and that they in fact already have. And while they do not yet claim the earthquakes will increase in strength, I am sure that is coming down the pike soon enough.

As the greatest power on the planet and the user of one-fourth of the earth's resources, it is, of course, primarily our fault that the earth is about to turn into a blazing ball of fire and that life as we know it will cease to exist. And just to hedge their bet, they have changed the name from global warming to climate change just in case the earth cools during the next one hundred years or so and results in an Ice Age instead, but it is the same dire threat.

Don't take my word for it. "Climate model projections summarized by the IPCC indicate that average global surface temperature will continue to rise during the 21st century by 1.1°C to 6.4°C. Such global warming will cause sea level to rise, and is expected to increase the intensity of extreme weather events and to change the amount/pattern of precipitation. Other effects of global warming include changes in agricultural yields, trade routes, glacier retreat, species extinctions and the increase in diseases" (http://www.kings.cam.ac.uk/library/global-warming-bibliography/). The only problem with these theories is that they have no foundation in fact.

Here's what we know for sure and I am about to give you some homework because if you have learned anything from me yet it is that I don't expect you to just take my word for it.

Fact: The earth has experienced increased and decreased temperatures throughout its long history. Most of these have been found in the fossil record and in ice cores taken around the world and most of them predate man's industrialization of the planet, meaning we were not responsible for it in the past.

Fact: Global temperatures have been steady for the last decade and in the last one hundred years we have experienced a slight warming of the planet to the tune of .4 degrees Celsius.

Not exactly the alarming increases promised just ten years ago. Remember, this increase applies to the last one hundred years.

Fact: Polar bear populations are on the rise in eleven of the thirteen populations identified by the world wildlife organizations.

Fact: The Alaskan Pipeline did not result in a drop in caribou herds; in fact, they increased.

Fact: Trees like carbon dioxide and actually use it to create oxygen for us to breathe.

Fact: Global warming is going to happen as a natural cycle of the earth's life and so will global cooling and there isn't a thing we can do about it, nor should we. It is a natural function of the planet and is most influenced by the cycles of the sun.

So where did I come by all this information, you ask? Simple—from the scientists around the world who actually study the independent areas in question and have written extensively about each of these situations, but who have, oddly, been ignored by the IPCC, the United Nations, and most of the environmental organizations that run off of government money.

Fact 1: The earth has experienced increased and decreased temperatures throughout its long history. Most of these have been found in the fossil record and in ice cores taken around the world and most of them predate man's industrialization of the planet, meaning we were not responsible for it in the past.

Here is a good place to start your personal research on the subject: http://www.worldclimatereport.com/index.php/ category/temperature-history/. This site has many articles written by real scientists working out in the field studying the very things that the IPCC believes to be true and are finding many of them to be false. The question is: "Is the UN lying to us, or have they just not made a complete study of the situation and jumped the gun a bit?" Well, I will leave that up to you for now.

The next place you can go (and I encourage you to look at any data you want to look at, but you must remember to look at each piece in context) is a site that will give you a list of even more places to go as you open your minds to learning about this: http://www.geocraft.com/WVFossils/ice_ages.html. This site gives you the information found in the IPCC report as well as many quotes from the high and mighty out there pushing the end of the world scenario.

And, finally, I have found this site to be quite educational: http://data.giss.nasa.gov/gistemp/. NASA seems to be a good place to learn the general stuff about the history of the planet's temperature.

Fact 2: Global temperatures have been steady for the last decade and in the last ten years we have experienced a slight warming of the planets to the tune of .4 degrees Celsius. Not exactly the alarming increases promised just ten years ago. Remember, this increase applies to the last one hundred years.

Check it out for yourself. In fact, go ahead and check out the last 140 years. http://www.cgd.ucar.edu/cas/catalog/climind/ TNI_N34/index.html#Sec5. I don't want to stop you from looking elsewhere so keep digging into this. But all the information I have found so far indicates the same thing: Nothing out of the ordinary is happening.

Fact 3: Polar bear populations are on the rise in eleven of the thirteen populations identified by the world wildlife organizations. And here is that information for you to ponder: http://www.csmonitor. com/2007/0503/p13s01-wogi.html. You will have to read the entire article to find the actual information, and I apologize for that. They do put the doom-and-gloom spin on it the best they can but if you are a savvy reader you will find just what I did. In case you need more information on it: http://www.polarbearsinternational.org/ask-the-experts/population/. And make sure to catch this line, which should be made at the start of any scientific study on any part of the global climate change debate, "First, it's important to note that scientists lack historical data on polar bear numbers—they only have rough estimates." At least they are honest.

Fact 4: The Alaskan Pipeline did not result in a drop in caribou population; in fact, they increased in numbers. This is often the argument made regarding anything we do to gain access to the oil in Alaska. But again, don't just believe me: http://www.wildlifenews.alaska.gov/index.cfm?adfg=wildlife_news.view_article&issue_id=13&articles_id=15. And additional information can be found here about the actual effect the pipeline has had on the population: http://sitemaker.umich.edu/section003_group001/home. I'd like to place special emphasis on the following sentence, "Since the pipeline was built, both of these herds have increased their numbers considerably. The data clearly indicates that the pipeline is not prohibiting caribou population growth or migration."

Fact 5: Trees like carbon dioxide and actually use it to create oxygen for us to breath: http://www.sciencedaily.com/releases/2009/08/090803173246.htm and http://earthobservatory.nasa.gov/Newsroom/view.php?id=22470. Just a side note on this one, it says that the scientists have released both ozone and carbon dioxide around the trees since 1997 when they were seedlings. If it is so dangerous, why add more of it to the atmosphere? Just a question …

Fact 6: Global warming is going to happen as a natural cycle of the earth's life and so will global cooling and there isn't a thing we can do about it, nor should we. It is a natural function of the planet.

And here it is, folks, the big answer to the big questions. What can we do about global warming? Should we even worry about it? The answer is no. We shouldn't worry about it because we can't do anything about it anyway; it is a natural cycle of the planet. This is not bad news for mankind.

The planet has shifted many times from a slightly warmer planet to a slightly cooler planet. There have been major ice ages and minor ones like the one that over took Europe in the 1600s. Ice-skating on the Thames in London was a common occurrence for a time. There have been heating trends that have made it a better place to grow crops up north and then a freeze making people relocate to other areas.

So what is the big push for global warming all about and why is America primarily considered the culprit in this dreamt-up scam? Well, the answer is twofold actually: Money is one reason and power or control would be the other.

You have to keep in mind that the United Nations is a government without a country to run. Essentially, the United Nations was set up to be a safe place for factions from different countries to come to talk with the hopes of avoiding another world war. Harry Truman said, at the time the United Nations was set up in San Francisco, "At no time in history has there been a more necessary meeting than this one … you members of this conference are to be architects of the better world. In your hands rests our future." And from that the United Nations started out with a simple plan to make the world a better place. At least that was the initial plan.

When the UN was set up it was set up with a few safeguards for the major powers in the world, namely, the United States, Great Britain, Russia (the Soviets), and China. These four held veto power over any ideas that came up in the UN and with just one of them a plan could be killed. This was established as a safety net so that no one set of principles would dominate the others. Consider this, Russia was communistic, as China was in the process of becoming, and Great Britain and the United States were essentially democracies. I say *essentially* because both have fallen into a more socialistic stance in modern times (which is something we all hope will change).

The UN was located in the US and I can only assume that is because we were the first to pony up the land for it and we also agreed to provide a majority of the financing for the organization, considering we were the country least affected by the war on the ground since it was fought "over there" and not here, except for Hawaii. So we enter into this little deal and we allowed forty some odd other countries to come along for the ride and all they had to do was want peace. This was great news for the world at large, right?

It would have been had they stuck to the charter, which was basically to provide a forum for countries to meet and discuss differences, genuinely try to help the economically poor countries come into the twentieth century with farming techniques to feed their people and better energy and water production techniques, and to bring a generalized feeling of goodwill toward the planet as a whole. The UN has no standing army and that is because the idea was that if any member was attacked the others would put up some troops to defend them if they could not defend themselves. And that idea lasted for about ten minutes, right up until the start of the Cold War, which arose from the spoils of World War II. So with the Soviets as charter members of the UN, what were we prepared to do, in reality, to stop them from expansion? We were going to use that all-powerful veto we shared to stop them if they tried anything funny. And since they ran every idea through the UN it worked out great (read sarcasm into that if you didn't already).

What actually happened was the Soviets ignored the very body they helped create except when there was a chance to use their veto to stop the US and Great Britain from doing anything about their violent expansion in Eastern Europe. They soaked up satellite countries like a sponge for a few years then decided to go for Germany herself with the blockade of Berlin. It was at this point that the term *Iron Curtain* was first coined by Winston Churchill as he pronounced, "An Iron Curtain has descended across Europe." And still the UN was powerless to do anything about it because of the veto power the Soviets held equal to ours.

As time moved forward the US did do what needed to be done by taking unilateral action (that just means we did what we had to do without anyone else when we needed to) to block Soviet expansion around the world. This is the reason for both our involvement in the Korean War and the Vietnam War. We fought less for the freedom of others than in an effort to stop the Soviets. Regardless of what the history books tell you, this is the real reason for our actions and justly so.

A few decades later the Soviet Union failed, thanks to the United States and Great Britain's policies of containment, and most of those countries split off again and were allowed to enter the UN and for the most part the world was safe for democracy to spread. Many countries turned over a new leaf or threw off the bonds that had held them back and flourished, even throwing off Mother Russia for a time. It was about this time the liberal mentality of the 1960s finally started getting into powerful positions both here at home and in the UN.

The UN is made up of many smaller counsels or committees. Some deal with energy, others with human rights, and still others with arms sales and international agreement enforcement. By and large though, to this day, the United States is still the power that gives the UN whatever strength it has with enforcement of any agreements.

Today, however, the United Nations seem to be getting ready to bite the hand that feeds it. By taking the charter to its extremes, it has decided the flawed scientific conclusions in the IPCC report is something that it should now attempt to force down the throats of every person on earth.

In December of 2009 a meeting in Copenhagen, Denmark, was scheduled to sign a new international treaty dealing with carbon emissions that would have affected the United States of America more than any other country on earth. All indications at the time seemed to indicate that the UN fully expected President Obama to sign the treaty as is. He didn't which is because of the people raising a little hell and a few Congressmen asking questions. You know how they love questions.

This treaty would tie the hands of the US on its use of the technology that creates $CO_2$ emissions. This treaty is even more threatening than the Cap and Trade Tax that has yet to hit the US economy (read up on it because it will affect you, too). This means coal plants that produce nearly half of all electricity in this country will either have to be shut down or revamped to meet, not the US definition of a clean-burning plant, but the United Nations definition of one. It will affect the mileage required in our automobiles. Mileage will need to be increased, which on the face of it doesn't sound so bad until you realize that the only way to do that in many cases is to make vehicles lighter, which makes them more dangerous. Good-bye, SUV. Hello, Smart Car–sized cars everywhere. While I have no issue with the smaller cars if people want them in this country, I should not have to drive one if I do not want one. I am rather fond of my Tahoe, not to mention a tad bit safer in it.

It will affect us most, however, in the pocketbook. The new treaty has in it the following that we need to be wary of:

## Excerpts from the Copenhagen Treaty

*Page 18:*

*36. The new agreed post-2012 institutional arrangement and legal framework to be established for the implementation, monitoring, reporting and verification of the global cooperative action for mitigation, adaptation, technology and financing, should be set under the Convention. It should include a financial mechanism and a facilitative mechanism drawn up to facilitate the design, adoption and carrying out of public policies, as the prevailing instrument, to which the market rules and related dynamics should be subordinate, in order to assure the full, effective and sustained implementation of the Convention. Basic pillars: government; facilitative mechanism; and financial mechanism, and the basic organization of which will include the following:*

*(a) The government will be ruled by the COP with the support of a new subsidiary body on adaptation, and of an Executive Board responsible for the management of the new funds and the related facilitative processes and bodies. The current Convention secretariat will operate as such, as appropriate.*

*FCCC/AWGLCA/2009/INF.2*

*Page 19*

*(b) The Convention's financial mechanism will include a multilateral climate change fund including five windows: (a) an Adaptation window, (b) a Compensation window, to address loss and damage from climate change impacts, including insurance, rehabilitation and compensatory components, (c) a Technology window; (d) a Mitigation window; and (e) a REDD window, to support a multi-phases process for positive forest incentives relating to REDD actions.*

*(c) The Convention's facilitative mechanism will include: (a) work programmes for adaptation and mitigation; (b) a long-term REDD process; (c) a short-term technology action plan; (d) an expert group on adaptation established by the subsidiary body on adaptation, and expert groups on mitigation, technologies and on monitoring, reporting and verification; and (e) an international registry for the monitoring, reporting and verification of compliance of emission reduction commitments, and the transfer of technical and financial resources from developed countries to developing countries. The secretariat will provide technical and administrative support, including a new centre for information exchange.*

*\*\*\*\*\*\*4. The Parties, in recognizing the need for greater efforts to adapt to climate change, agree to further enhance the implementation of their common obligations under Article 4.1(e) of the Convention.*

*Page 69 12. Definitions, modalities, rules and guidelines for the treatment of land use, land use change and forestry under the Kyoto Protocol shall apply to all (developed country Parties).*

*(All developed country Parties and countries that are voluntarily wish to be treated as developed countries shall adopt legally binding mitigation commitments or actions.)*

*Page 70 : Alternative 4 to paragraph 17:*

*All developed country Parties (shall) adopt legally binding mitigation commitments including economy-wide quantified emission reduction objectives for the period from (2013) until 2020, while ensuring comparability of efforts among them, taking into account differences in their national circumstances.*

*Excerpts continued:*

*P.P.10 (Emphasizing that) it is fundamental that Annex I countries comply fully with the provisions as set out in 4.3, 4.4, and 4.5 as well as additional commitments on technology transfer and capacity-building.*

*P.P.11 (Further emphasizing that) a shared vision does not include commitments for developing countries. It does, entitle technology transfer, capacity-building and financial resources for project implementation regarding mitigation national programs.*

*P.P.13 Recognizing that current and potential climate change impacts require a shift in the global investment patterns and that criteria for financing allocation shall clearly respond to the priorities identified by the international community, with climate change stabilization being one of these priorities.*

*P.P.14 Acknowledging that current atmospheric concentrations are principally the result of historical emissions of greenhouse gases, the most significant share of which has originated in developed countries.*

*P.P.15 Further acknowledging that developed countries have a historical responsibility for their disproportionate contribution to the causes and consequences of climate change, reflecting their disproportionate historical use of a shared global carbon space since 1850 as well as their proposed continuing disproportionate use of the remaining global carbon space.*

*8. Deep cuts (by developed countries) (by all Annex I country Parties) (by all developed countries) in global*

*emissions by Parties in accordance with their historical
responsibilities, as well as the principles
        FCCC/AWGLCA/2009/INF.2*

Allow me to translate for you: Americans will pay a bunch
through their tax dollars to the UN in exchange for continuing
to live the life they live and that money will be spread around
the globe to all manner of third world countries where it can be
squandered by local warlords and other political crooks. Thanks,
hardworking American, you are swell!!

Now, had this been signed it would still need to be approved
by the Senate as they are charged with this power under Article II,
Section 2, and Clause 2 of the US Constitution. This article deals
directly with the president in the executive office and how he may
enter the country into treaties, "He shall have Power, *by and with
the Advice and Consent of the Senate, to make Treaties, provided
two thirds of the Senators present concur.*" While the president
may be gung ho about the idea of stopping global warming when
the case has not been proven to even exist beyond the normal
fluctuations of the planet, we can hopefully count on the Senate
to protect and defend the Constitution and thereby the people of
the United States. Then again, Harry Reid leads the Senate with
his legion of fifty-nine other Democratic senators, making sixty
votes toward the sixty-seven needed to "consent," so it is anyone's
guess. But I am willing to bet we have a much better chance of
stopping this if you pick up the phone, fire up the fax machine,
and light up your senatorial member's e-mail account.

If you have picked up on the mixed message of this treaty
you are right. Just because Obama did not sign it this time
doesn't mean he won't next trip. Another reason we need to
stay vigilant.

I think you might have a slightly better understanding of
the situation we face in this country today regarding climate
change and the United Nations. But I can only stress this so
many times, please do not take my word for it. You need to
read up on the subject because it concerns you, it concerns

your children, and it concerns the taxes that you and your kids will be forced to pay in the future to finance something that is not even administered by this country.

Here is the part that burns me up personally the most about this entire situation. The United States has the power to stop this with one simple veto of the entire situation. China won't veto it because they are exempt, which means they can pollute to high heaven without paying a dime to the UN, as is India and a number of high-population emerging countries. You think Russia will veto it? Seriously doubt that happening because like it or not we are still in a war of ideology with Russia all these years later as they move slowly back to a state domination of everything in that nation again. And don't count on Great Britain to save the day either. Their diplomats are pushing this idea nearly as strong as the UN itself.

Get educated and get active. Submission to world government is not in our wheelhouse.

# Chapter 8

How do we fix America?

Well, the first step is understanding what the rules we have to operate under are. Education in this country, as we have discussed, is pitiful. So, unlike some people who write terrific books about the issues of the day, I am not going to assume you know how the system works. First, I'm going to take you through a few pages so that you understand how the pieces fit together.

First of all, we are not forced to live in a top-down system where the federal government is on top, the states on the next tier, followed by the countries, cities, and finally the citizen.

Flip it in your mind. We hold the power, the citizen. The Constitution was originally written to recognize our equality with the king of England, the country from which we broke away. Our rights are not bestowed upon us by the Constitution. They are natural and self-evident, conferred through the amazing self-awareness of creation, resulting in enlightened self-interest, which drives free market economies to higher prosperity than any system in human history. We are the kings of this nation, and all levels of government, from the city council to the president of the United States of America, work for us. Not the other way around.

Take a minute than think about that. You are a king or queen. Seriously! You live in the only nation on earth where your rights are protected by a document not giving them to you, but limiting the government's rights to take them from you or interfere with your life. If you don't find that incredible, you probably should not go on because what I am about to tell you will just piss you off.

While our rights are made secure by the Constitution, on our own we have very little power. Our true power comes when we unite behind an idea. This is what led to the creation of the many states in the first place; people of like mind coming together to give life to an idea where none existed before.

All thirteen of the original states predate the federal government, most by decades. It was the representatives of these states that came together to breathe life into the federal government. In their wisdom they understood they were creating a possible monster so they wrote the Constitution to limit the federal government's scope of power and to protect the states and the citizens who resided therein.

In the back of this book you will find the Constitution as originally ratified with the original first ten amendments known as the Bill of Rights and all subsequent amendments that were added over the years. The Constitution describes the role of the federal government and the way in which it would be set up. The first ten amendments were added shortly after to make sure that the citizens were protected and that the rights of the states were protected as well. This was what Thomas Jefferson referred to as the "Experiment" that representative government would be.

That is another thing we need to touch on real quick. We do not live in a democracy although you might think we do. A true democracy would have us voting on every bill ourselves and the majority would simply rule the day until such time that another law passed by the people overrides that older one. Humanity does not have enough time to run itself by a democracy, to be quite frank with you. So it was decided that we would create a republic whereby we invest certain powers that are ours alone to other individuals to act on our behalf on matters of governance. Think of it as power of attorney. When we elect our representatives we empower them to make certain decisions on our behalf. This is why it is important that we vote in elections, to make sure that those who are going to represent our geographic location are chosen by the highest possible number of people so those who are governed can be reasonably sure that their representative will act in their interests. This is essentially what we do with all our public servants. We are lending them the power we have for a limited time period to work on our behalf. This includes the police and sheriff departments. We elect the people who pass the laws that the police must enforce. We do this because, again, we don't have the time to run around enforcing the laws the people passed. We hire these people to do that job for us. This is not socialism as some have suggested, this is merely recognition that we are busy people and need someone to focus on these areas for us.

So how does it all work?

Let's start with the local elections first. From dogcatchers to judges, there are many things locally that we do not have time to do, so we hire others to do it for us. These are your basic civil servants. They are Americans who wish to serve the public so they throw their name in the hat to do so. They often have years of experience in certain fields that they believe will make them well suited to oversee these areas of government on our behalf. A lawyer might run for a judgeship, a home builder might run for planning committee for a town, or a former police officer might run for dogcatcher as he knows well the laws he enforced for years. These all make sense and most often these people do a fine job of representing us on that level. And if they don't, we simply replace them in a few years, call for a recall election to remove them, and run ourselves to replace them.

Next are your city supervisors. They are elected to run the municipality that you live in. They make sure the potholes get fixed in the street and that the traffic lights work right. Some cities are larger than others and get involved in all manner of governance, like homeless shelters that may or may not have both state and federal funding involved but are still run by the local city in most cases. But, again, we invest in them certain powers to make decisions for us. If we don't like what they do, we remove them.

Down the ladder a little further we come to the county supervisors. They pass laws regarding larger areas that might involve a few towns or cities in their sphere of influence. Many times pissing matches break out between city and county governments, especially if there is one dominant city within a county. This is just how it goes. Both are supposed to be battling it out to make the best decision possible based on your vote that put them there. They usually work it out. When they do not, they take their cases to the courts. We will discuss them and their hierarchy in a bit.

Lower still we find the states. Here we have the culmination of the desires of all the voters in a state. Each state has its own individual constitution that it must abide by, but all basically say the same thing; they are there to protect your rights and to provide a place for the collective governance of the geographic area. They are the highest authority in that geographic area and as such, they have a good deal of the peoples' power invested in them.

At the lowest possible rung of the ladder of who runs this country we find the federal government. Now this might sound strange to many of you because it seems as if they run the show most of the time. Well, as we talked about in Chapter 1, this is because they have usurped so much of the power from the states that it appears that way. But remember, the federal government was the creation of the many states, not the other way around.

Inside the federal government is where we find the culmination of all that has gone wrong with this country. The very way the rules have been written makes it unlikely that anyone, even the most well-spoken constitutional scholar, could explain all of its inner workings so that any average American could fully understand it. What we are going to do is start here at the federal level and work our way back up to the top: YOU.

Now we know who the players are, let's look at how it all works together to make your life either good or bad.

The federal government is broken up into three branches of government. Each one of these is designed to provide checks and balances to the other two. You remember this from school, I'm sure. But what you may not understand is exactly what each one is supposed to do, in comparison to what it actually does do.

First up, let's look at the legislative branch, or Congress. Article 1 of the United States Constitution spells out the details of what this group is charged with doing. As I mentioned earlier, the Constitution is in the back of the book so feel free to compare and decide for yourself if you think they are holding true to the intent of the Constitution.

The United States Congress is broken up into two distinct groups or houses. One is called the Senate and the other is called the House of Representatives. It is from here that all legislation or laws come. Every single law we have in this country has been developed in these two chambers and usually at the same time. Here's how it works.

Somebody has a bright idea; usually a group of people bring to the attention of a Representative or Senator some urgent situation that needs to be legislated in their mind. The citizen or group writes a piece of legislation or bill and tries to get whichever congressman whey have the ear of to bring it to the floor for a vote or they try to get the congressman to write a bill to bring to the floor. The House votes, the Senate votes, and it goes to the president to sign it into law or it fails to pass and is gone forever. Seems simple, doesn't it? Well, it would be if that's how it worked.

Here's what really tends to happen. Somewhere in America a special interest group meets to decide what kind of legislation is necessary to benefit their company, group, or industry. Now, don't be upset by the name "special interest group"; this is what any group would be called that had a particular interest. Veterans, vacuum cleaner salesmen, mothers against drunk drivers, the NAACP, insurance companies, or automakers—it doesn't matter what group you are talking about, they all have a special interest in something and the government is where you can go to try to change America one way or the other.

So in comes ABC Group with a proposed bill to make XYZ illegal. Remember, all our rights were established early on so if the government is going to pass a bill, it is always to take something away from you, *always*, with the only exception being if they give something back that they earlier took and enough people raised hell about it. Otherwise, remember that point: Government always takes; it never gives, *never*. It will never give you a right. It might give one back, but it never creates a right anywhere, from anything, or for anyone. They may, however, create "Entitlements," which become obfuscated as "Rights." Social Security, Medicare, Welfare, and others, just to name a few.

ABC Group starts shopping the bill around Washington DC to see if anyone is interested in supporting their idea. The people shopping the bill are those lobbyists we hear so much about. They are lobbying for a vote in their direction or for a piece of legislation to be brought up that would benefit their group or the group they are representing on Capitol Hill. There is no other reason to lobby Congress, ever, except to try to influence a vote. Anyone who suggests differently is flat-out lying to you. This does not make them bad people; it's just their job in most cases and it is the way things have always been done. In today's society, we have refined it to an art form.

They find Congressman Smith and he agrees to look into the situation or agrees to offer support. Now, he might have done so out of a real passion for the subject, or he might have been offered a hefty campaign contribution to assist them in this matter. Either way, it is almost impossible to tell, as many of these congressmen get yearly contributions from many companies on both sides of any number of issues. Quite often they are just reminded of contributions in the past, which don't necessarily have to be made in the future, but rarely that directly.

In Congress, no one person can just make it happen, it's all about consensus. You have to first build a coalition to help you move the bill through the system, and every bill gets its first rundown in a committee. Committees decide when a bill is ready to be voted on by the whole of the Congress, either in the

House or Senate. So Smith takes the bill to his committee first. You might ask why. Because more than likely it is because of the committee he sits on that he was even approached by ABC Group with the idea in the first place. First rule of sales (or lobbying): "Know who the decision makers are and don't waste your time with people who can't buy or make something happen."

These committees are tremendously powerful entities on the Hill. You have a ton of them and each one has a chairman. Here's the catch to that idea, the chairman is almost always a member of the majority party in Congress. So if the Democrats have more people in the House than the Republicans, guess who sits as chairman on every committee in the House? A Democrat. And over in the Senate, if Republicans control the majority of Senate seats, then Republicans are the chairman of every Senate committee. This comes from the old Roman adage "to the victors go the spoils of war." It makes sense, I guess, considering that every time we have an election in this country and there is a change in majority the new guys have a chance to get in there deep and make real change happen. Yeah, right!

These committee members are chosen after each election cycle. Obviously, if you don't get reelected you no longer have a seat on any committee, let alone Congress. But imagine you were placed (there is no voting for committee members, you are appointed by the chairman or as part of a deal to gain access to certain other committees) on a committee during your first term in office. Usually the ranking or most senior member of the majority party is the chair of the committee. People fight for decades to get this title, like Charlie Rangel, the current chair of the Ways and Means Committee in the Senate. This is the committee from which all tax code legislation comes. Imagine the power. So each time the Democrats take power they try to add members to all the committees and then every time the Republicans take the majority they do the same. Some of these appointments are in hopes of a chairmanship decades later. This is real long-range planning by these guys; too bad they don't think like that about the business they are supposed to be taking care of.

Smith is the chairman of the committee or is of the same party as the chairman. Face it, if they are of the other party and the chairman decides what gets talked about, what are the chances that a member of the other party is going to get something through the committee at all? Those members of the other party are biding their time until the next time their party is in power. Did you think they were there to provide balance? Not a chance. The committees write their own rules so the chairman can change what it takes to get a bill out of committee in the first place, which means the party in power is the party in power. Don't let them ever fool you with this "obstructionist other party" crap unless the majorities are really tight. Take, for instance, the situation in the House and Senate today. The Democratic Party controls a complete supermajority in the Senate with sixty votes to the Republicans' forty votes. Those sixty votes are the ultimate majority and the Republicans cannot do anything about it. In the House the Democrats enjoy a massive majority of some forty to fifty seats. This means the Republicans would have to win forty to fifty in the House just to equal the Democrats, and no less than eleven to gain control of the Senate. Democrats run this government today, lock, stock, and barrel.

Smith gets the bill on the roster and over the next few months they work on recruiting allies in the Senate. He will need them because the Senate will have to draft its own version of the bill. So Smith finds some help from Senator Jones who sits on the corresponding committee in the Senate and together the two committees begin drafting all kinds of stuff into the original bill.

Some time ago another senator tried to get a bill through that dealt with helping catfish farmers in Arkansas (because they make huge donations to her) but it got defeated in the floor vote or was vetoed by the president (more on that in a bit) so the bill died. This other senator talks Jones into adding it as a line item in the new bill so that it will be piggybacking on this bill when the vote comes down later. This is called a rider or pork. It is a dead idea that sees a second life as part of a new bill. The other name for this is earmarks. Recently there have been many promises to stop this kind of earmarking by both parties, but it has yet to happen.

After a few months or several years in committees (oh yes, some of these bills take years to get through committee) the House and Senate both pass their respective versions of the bill. But this doesn't make it law yet. Now it has to go to a joint subcommittee and be reconciled, or put together with matching language. These two bills must now become one. This is where the real action can happen. Oftentimes it is at this point that the real meat of a bill gets gutted or made stronger. They take the parts they like (by *them* I mean the committee members of this joint committee of which Smith and Jones are both members) and they hash out every line of it. It is where earmarks are dropped and, all too often, added. After all this positioning and counterpositioning the bill is presented one more time to both the House and Senate for a final floor vote where it either passes or it doesn't. Most likely, having gone this far, it will make it through. Of course, the bill may hardly resemble the original idea that was brought to Smith years or months earlier, as concessions had to be made to get the votes to pass it. The catfish pork is there, but another House member's abortion funding got cut in order to pick up a few conservative votes and a small defense spending appropriation was added to shore up those conservative votes, too.

Did I mention that the original bill (we will call it House Resolution HR001 and Senate Resolution SR001) was brought by the Coalition for Healthy Eating and all they wanted was for labels on food to show the amounts of foreign product in the package so people would know if they were buying food products from foreign countries? You laugh and wonder what defense spending, abortion, and catfish farming have to do with a bill that gives country of origin information, but don't laugh; this is exactly the kind of stuff that gets stuffed into bills all the time.

This is as good a representation as any of the process that happens in the Congress every day. Deals, deals, and more deals ... that is the order of the day, every day. And for the most part it used to work out pretty well. These days, however, the amounts of money being moved around the chessboard are astronomical. Millions were replaced with billions and billions now seem small compared to the trillions the country owes as national debt.

Then there is the Congress's other job, oversight. They are to provide oversight for both the judicial and executive branches. What this means with the judicial branch is that they confirm federal justices or judges to their benches for life or for the term prescribed by law. These folks are nominated by the president and brought to the Senate for advice and consent, the wonderful little term that would make you think everyone is working together in order to get the best people in the job. Usually, however, in a situation where the president is of one party and the Senate dominated by the other, it becomes a pissing match and a place where smears and slurs become the order of the day. Today it actually has a name: "Borking." When Ronald Reagan was president he nominated Judge Robert Bork for the Supreme Court and sent his name to the Senate. Bork had a history and had worked for President Nixon years earlier and was a latecomer to the scandal that put Nixon on a plane back to California. Bork actually fired the investigators involved, so some Democrats (who controlled the Senate at the time) were working for a payback. At the time, Senator Ted Kennedy was on the Judiciary Committee (again, a committee to start the process before anything goes to the full Senate for a vote—it is important to know the House of Representatives play no role constitutionally in this process, only the Senate), and they held the customary committee hearings involving Judge Bork. This is kind of like an interview with the committee. Robert Bork sat before the committee and Ted Kennedy took him apart with one false statement after another, literally destroying the man's reputation by suggesting a world in which Bork on the Supreme Court would drive women to back-alley abortions, Blacks to the back of the bus again, and all manner of horrible things. The term being "Borked" was born. In the end the Senate voted not to "consent" to Judge Bork serving on the Supreme Court's bench.

This extends to many members of the president's staff. Congress is charged with oversight of the executive branch itself, that being the president. They are to again "advise and consent" certain cabinet-level positions and make sure that the president spends the money they appropriate correctly. They can do this by calling hearings in any of the multitude of committees they have in Congress. Seems simple enough, but how can anyone say for sure where $2.8 trillion goes every year? I mean, really. They have investigation after investigation and periodically they catch a few billion dollars going here or there when it shouldn't have. But in the end, there is little they can do to control it. It's just so incredibly huge and the government today is just too damn big to control with any real prospect of reducing waste, at least until people really dedicated to just that very action are elected.

The second branch spelled out by the US Constitution is the executive branch, better known as the presidency. The founders of this country were so concerned about executive power that just like Article 1 spelled out the legislative branch's responsibilities, Article 2 spells out exactly what the president's job is and is not to be. Take a gander at it and make the call for yourself if the current president or any in history are upholding its provisions.

The president has a few jobs, among them he is the Commander in Chief of the US military when we are at war, he is the main law enforcement office in the nation, and he administers the programs that use the public treasury.

Let's go back to our bills that we passed earlier, HR001 and SR001, which have now been combined and passed as US001. They are presented to the president for his signature. He has choices to make here. He can sign the bill into law immediately or he can veto the bill and send it back to Capitol Hill for them to tweak it to his liking. There is one other thing he can do, of course: He can let it sit on his desk until it becomes law automatically by nature of his inaction. This is the easy way out for a president who knows that whether he signs it or vetoes it, he is going to catch hell for it. It is popular when the House and Senate are closely split.

If he signs it, it becomes law. The deed is done unless someone with standing before the court brings a suit to the courts to find either parts of the new law or the entire law to be unconstitutional. We will handle that in a bit when we discuss the judiciary.

If the president vetoes the bill it can go one of a few ways. Congress can take it back and try to make it more to his liking, or they can see if they have the votes to overturn the veto, which takes a 60 percent vote in the House and Senate. Remember that number sixty from earlier? That is the number Democrats currently have in the Senate, creating the supermajority so called because they can make anything law so long as they keep all sixty Senators voting the same way. However, in order to override a presidential veto they need two-thirds of the vote in both houses of Congress. But that means only pulling a few from the other side of the aisle. And that massive majority in the House of Representatives also controlled by the Democrats? Same situation, although they don't quite have the supermajority needed to guarantee the veto gets overturned either; however, they are close enough that with just a little cajoling of a few of the more liberal Republicans, they can pretty much get it done. Of course, this is really just academic considering a Democrat is in the White House as well and the chances are if a bill hits his desk passed by a Democratic Congress, he's going to sign it because he probably asked for it. Consider this when thinking about the healthcare bills moving through Congress right now. President Obama is their biggest fan. Whatever comes out of committee and the floor vote, he will probably sign.

If the bill does get vetoed and Congress overturns the veto, it becomes law despite the president's opinion or action against it. This is the "checks and balances" at work. Although not an everyday occurrence, it has happened plenty of times in our history. There is one idea that has bounced around Washington for years that never quite seems to go away and that is the idea of a presidential line item veto. It would give the president the ability to simply veto a line of a bill, like the catfish funding, while leaving the rest of the bill intact before signing it into law. It seems every party in power likes the idea while every one out of power hates it. Both of their arguments make sense.

As commander in chief, the president is also the head of the military. Although most day-to-day operations are handled by the generals, the Pentagon, and the Department of Defense, the president gives the direction on the big picture. The president brings a declaration of war to Congress, where they vote to go to war or not. These days that part of the Constitution is quite muddied by precedent to the contrary with Vietnam, Korea, and the current Afghanistan and Iraq wars being undertaken with Congress's approval more of an afterthought. Speaking constitutionally, the president is not supposed to go to war without a declaration of war from Congress. During times of war this is perhaps the most important job the president has as he swore to "defend the Constitution from all enemies, foreign and domestic."

His day-to-day job is really to enforce the law. The president has at his disposal a cabinet. The cabinet members represent various areas of government. From foreign relations, which is handled by the State Department, to education and the Department of Education, money is handled by the Treasury Department, etc. The number of cabinet positions isn't set by the Constitution and it has grown over the last 225-plus years to cover all sorts of things. Homeland Security is the newest member of the group.

Each cabinet-level position is filled by a person approved through the "advise and consent" of Congress, but once in place, these people work at the will of the president. They run the different departments based on the president's desires. They spend the funds dedicated to them by Congress and advise the president on different issues that need attention. It is because of these advisors and administrators that the president may request Congress to make a law or consider making a law to deal with certain situations.

You may hear the term *Czar* from time to time. These are really just special advisors who don't need the Congress's confirmation and who also advise the president. They are not cabinet-level people, they oversee no part of the US budget, but they can be highly influential to the president's decision-making process. This is why many do not care for people in these positions being so close to a sitting president when they have not been through the Senate confirmation process. Little is known about these people in many cases, and this can cause tension and distrust. The term is nothing new; Ronald Reagan had a drug Czar who advised him on Drug Interdiction Policy (Bob Bennett), but he was one of very few. Bill Clinton had a dozen or so, but most had very limited scopes of influence. President Obama has taken this nonconfirmed, federally funded position to new heights, with thirty-six Czars at last count "advising" him on everything from green jobs to environmental policy. One major concern has been the apparent duplication of advisors. President Obama has a green jobs Czar and a secretary of commerce, a secretary of education and an education Czar, a secretary of treasury and a stimulus monies Czar. So the question begs to be asked, "Is it the Senate-confirmed cabinet members that sway the president the most, or his handpicked choices that were not confirmed by the Senate and as such have never been vetted?" Van Jones, anyone? If you don't know the name, I highly suggest you Google it.

The final branch of the federal government to be addressed is the judicial branch. In Article 3 the courts' responsibilities are spelled out rather plainly. However, whereas today we consider all three branches of federal government to be equal in power, it wasn't always like that. Originally the Supreme Court was only to refer back questionable legislation or law to Congress for them to fix or to the president for him to deal with. Striking down law as "unconstitutional" evolved over time. Today many argue the Supreme Court wields the ultimate power. While operating as a check on the other two branches it can and has usurped some powers to legislate from the bench by upholding or creating law out of whole cloth. *Roe v. Wade*, *Brown v. Board of Education*, and others have changed the country immensely without ever having gone through Congress or the president to be debated or signed into law. Both created law where none existed previously. And, while many will suggest that both granted rights previously unknown, neither did, as both eliminated the right of the people to be fully represented by their duly elected representatives. As I said earlier, government never gives you a right; it only takes them away or restricts them.

When a lawsuit is filed it usually does not start at the Supreme Court but at the lower federal court level or even in the states. Let's go back to US001, our mythical law requiring food labels to show their country of origins and percentages of foreign filler.

LMN Company files a lawsuit against XYZ Corporation stating that they are not following the law by showing that some of its food comes from Puerto Rico. WXY files a countersuit to stop the introduction of US001 into their processing plants in Puerto Rico, being that it is a US territory. The federal court in Florida says that even though Puerto Rico is a territory of the US, it brings in foodstuffs from foreign countries that it then sends to the mainland so it must therefore be accounted for under the new law. XYX Corp. isn't pleased with this so they file an appeal to the Federal Appeals Court and it is then heard by them. The Appeals Court overturns the federal court decision and says XYZ isn't responsible for the product that gets to Puerto Rico, only that which comes from Puerto Rico, and since it is a territory of the US, it does not have to report it as a foreign source.

Now LMN isn't happy with the reversal so it takes the case to the top, the Supreme Court of the United States. Now, the Supreme Court has a choice. They can take the case now, they can delay taking it until their next session, which could be a year away, or they can refuse to take the case altogether, thus making the last judgment the new precedent by which all future cases will be compared when dealing with this subject.

All the Supreme Court is charged with doing in reality is ensuring that the laws passed by Congress and signed by the president pass constitutional muster. Some might consider them the last line of defense while others see them as the first line of attack, thus bypassing the usual hearings and endless committees and presidential politics that oftentimes come to bear on legislation and drag it out and delay changes. Simply having the Supreme Court say something is or is not constitutional oftentimes makes legislation ineffective from the start.

That covers the basics that you need to understand about how the federal government operates today. There are literally a hundred-plus committees on the Hill today and you could write a separate book on what each one does and how they operate within the government as a whole.

In the good old days, people brought ideas to Congress, and once in a while it still happens, but today's politics are run less by the people and more by the lobbyists and that is our fault. We gave that power away. Here's a little-known secret: WE CAN TAKE IT BACK!

The states operate in much the same way. Although each has a different individual constitution by which they govern themselves, each must keep in accordance with the US Constitution. No state can pass a law that is counterintuitive to federal law. This means that if Nevada says that gambling is legal, it is only because the federal government has never passed a law saying it is illegal. This applies to prostitution as well. There is no federal law prohibiting prostitution; therefore, it is legal unless otherwise legislated locally. Now within Nevada, for instance, in Clark County, the county that encompasses Las Vegas, prostitution is illegal. But it's not in the surrounding counties. Again notice that government, regardless of the level of government, only takes away rights, it does not give them. This is the essence of all governmental legislation. As you move up the chain of responsibility from you to the federal government (notice I said chain of accountability, not chain of command or responsibility) no level below can pass a law that counters a law passed above it. So no county can pass a law that goes against the grain of a state law and no state can pass a law that goes against the grain of federal law.

Are you starting to understand what President Jefferson meant when he said, "Government which governs least, governs best"?

All states have a governor and all of the states have individual houses of state legislation although they go by different names. In fact, not all states call themselves states, many call themselves commonwealths. But at the end of the day they are all on equal footing when it comes to dealing with the citizens of the states and in their relationship with the federal government.

All states also have a state court system with a state Supreme Court. These state courts must adhere to federal court decisions and cannot decide that something found to be unconstitutional by the federal court is constitutional at the state level. This again is power we gave the federal government when we created it, a way to make sure that common laws apply equally across the country. This is why if you are married in Arizona your marriage is legally binding in Michigan. This is also one of the reasons gay or same-sex marriage is causing such a fit in the country. If Maine and Hawaii pass a law saying that marriage is legal in their state for same-sex couples, by law all of the other forty-eight states must recognize it, too, even if their local laws prohibit it. The federal courts have yet to weigh in on this subject; therefore, a major battle is brewing. Many at the federal level are trying to pass legislation or even pass a constitutional amendment making it illegal, but even with that, it will still have to pass constitutional muster in the Supreme Court to hold any real legal weight.

This is why the presidency is really important to the liberal and conservative parties. While a president will often serve only four years, eight if he or she (although it hasn't happened yet, I'm sure Americans will vote a woman into office at some point) is lucky, after that he is term limited out of office. But a Supreme Court member is appointed for a lifetime. We have members of the Court who were placed there under Reagan thirty years ago, and in Reagan's time, he was fighting a federal bench populated by Carter and Johnson appointees. Makes one think a bit more about the real power of the president to formulate for decades the way things will be handled even after he is out of office or even dead and buried.

At the local level, city and county, you have various commissions and committees again, but their scopes of influence are much more limited. You may have a mayor of a town within a county with whom the local sheriff may have to work, especially when dealing with the city police, who work for the mayor, but that sheriff himself may have been directly elected by the people. Sheriff Joe Arpaio in Maricopa County, Arizona, is a particular case of direct country election and he answers only to the state attorney general on the legality of what he does. He does not take direction from them. He runs the law enforcement under his control as he feels it is best to do so and follows only the Constitution in its execution. This drives many crazy, but with an 86 percent approval rating in the county, it is hard for anyone to argue with his methods. He is the result of direct elections.

Other local officials work to make sure the water is clean, the roads are maintained, and that crime is not a problem. They generally work for the county or city you live in and are a direct result of who you elected to hire them. They are your neighbors and usually where any complaints about community life will be listened to.

Finally, back to the top of the ladder we have you, the voter. Although there are certain powers and responsibilities you have instructed the various levels of government to execute on your behalf, this does not mean you have abdicated the responsibility for the actions of those to whom you have entrusted that power. As the king you have merely delegated authority, not abdicated responsibility. That line was told to me by a man named Al Richer for whom I once worked. He was talking about being a manager in his company, but it applies even more to citizenship in a free country.

Your job in the government is perhaps the most important of them all as citizenship is not a take it or leave it proposition. You are a king or queen and any king or queen who does not take an active role in the running of their country soon finds themselves removed from the throne.

We have only one real weapon or tool with which to rule our country and that is the vote. Although our elections are not without question at times, we have for the most part the most reliable election process on earth. That's sad to even say, "Although our elections are not without question." We gave the modern world the blueprint by which all other free nations reflect on their freedom. In every country around the world that has ever been freed from the tyranny of dictatorship or the grip of Communism, the vote has been the weapon used to hold at bay those forces that would otherwise trample the people again.

I have a few friends who came to America legally from other countries. They have all earned their citizenship and worked hard to pass the required test. Each of them understands the importance of the power they now wield as kings and queens of their new homeland, their new kingdom. They are better versed in the Constitution than any average American who was raised in the glow of the very freedom these people fought, in some cases, a lifetime to enjoy. Yet today the civics taught in elementary school and high school are not even as complete as this chapter of this book.

We see election results where people go on television and make statements about the new president making their mortgage payments, buying them a new car, or in some other way making their life better as if it is owed to them for some reason. Not to mention, none of those things are even within his ability to provide, which they would know if we had a solid civics education in the schools. In the early days of this republic you had to drag a good man into office kicking and screaming. Yet today, you can't get rid of a bad man in public office without the same kicking and screaming.

And that, my fellow average Americans, is your fault and mine. For the last fifty-plus years we have been asleep at the wheel. Oh, sure, we have awoken a few times from our slumber to make a course change or two, but for the most part we have slept while the country has been on what we thought was cruise control. "Nobody would challenge America's strength, our economy, and the greatness of wealth we have created through the free exercise of our economic and political freedom." This was the collective pronouncement by Americans for the last fifty years or more.

Today we find that our country is being passed in wealth by every other country on earth, as we hold a debt larger than any country in the world can even conceive. While we may not have been surpassed in military strength (and considering the poor state of affairs the former Soviet Union finds itself in today we may not be for another hundred years), what good can come if it cannot keep us safe from losing our homes to high interest rates and losing our jobs while our economy continues to fail because of government involvement more so than any outside forces placed upon it.

We put these people into these positions. When they were not doing what we wanted, we should have removed them.

But it is not too late. We can regain control of our country, but it isn't going to be easy. Wait, actually it will be easy, for the one thing we have not yet handed over is the very thing that makes us free. Our vote.

# Chapter 9

## The Vote and Taking America Back

A properly conducted vote is the fundamental difference between free countries and dictatorships. But consider this; the vote alone is worthless if you don't have choices to vote for. Just a year before the Second Gulf War or the Invasion of Iraq, whichever you want to call it, Saddam Hussein actually won reelection with a staggering 96 percent of the vote. Boy oh boy, did those people love the way Iraq was being governed or what? Imagine a 96 percent vote in America for anything at all. I am willing to bet that if you put a poll out asking what color the sky is you would be hard-pressed to get a 96 percent vote for blue if red was on the ballot as the only other option in this country.

The obvious question of a fixed election is glaring, but that isn't really the point. The point is a properly proposed ballot. In America today we operate on a basic two-party system of political parties, Democrats and Republicans, with some smaller ones thrown in for good measure, Greens, Libertarians, even an American Socialist and an American Communist party. But in reality, none of these smaller parties have the infrastructure to create a governing body on a national level. Imagine a president elected from a third party going to Capitol Hill without a single party member to support his or her ideas in Congress. They would be unbelievably ineffective, even more so than we have come to expect from our elected officials.

The sad thing about the current "third" parties in this country is that they don't seem to be grasping that concept. Here is the game plan for a third party to work: Start local and grow out. Get control of a state house then grow to a few state houses. Once that has been done make a play for a few governorships around the country. Then start populating the Senate and House of Representatives. Once you have a 20 percent stake in state and national politics run a real presidential candidate like Ron Paul who understands the ramifications of carrying such a huge debt load in this country and who understands the importance of the founding documents on which this country was built.

An even better idea for them is to repopulate the existing parties and remake them from the inside out. While there are some major differences between the party platforms as they expose them, when it comes to governance it can be hard to tell the differences. Republicans or the GOP will tell you they are fiscally conservative while spending more during the George W. Bush years than any previous administration. Then along come the Democrats saying that Bush spent too much and off they go on a spending spree that dwarfs the Bush years three to one.

The GOP tells you that we need to go to war in Afghanistan because of the Taliban's protection of Bin Laden, and it will take time to win the fight. Then they fail to offer the support the troops need to get the job done with manpower and equipment. Along come the Democrats with a promise to remove the troops altogether with a deadline that reveals our will to the enemy in some range, depending on which speech you play back. Yet, instead of doing that they are talking about expanding the war with another forty thousand troops. I'm not taking a side on the war effort except to say that if we are going to fight a war, we had best do so with the intention of winning it. This flip-flopping all over the board is showing our very real enemies out there just how divided we can be on things. A quick and decisive war is always our best policy if it comes to that.

It appears that the one thing they definitely have in common is an inability to either tell us the truth or see the whole issue prior to speaking to us. Either way, the choices have left most Americans with something of a poor taste in our mouths when it comes to politics. But again, whose fault is that? Yours and mine for letting them get used to treating us like children and not holding them accountable for their failures when they happen. If you've ever raised kids, and I have, you know that you get out of your kids what you expect. If you expect them to be great, they will be. If you don't have expectations of performance in school, sports, dance, whatever they are into, you will get exactly what you expect: mediocrity. Don't believe me? Please look at exhibit A; a national government held to the lowest of expectations delivering the lowest of results while running up the largest debt in the history of the planet.

Now the question becomes: "To whom can we best offer the choices needed to elect good people to office?" Well, the best people I can think of are the people reading this book right now. Hi there, Mr. or Mrs. Future Leader of your country. I'm talking to YOU!

Freaky, isn't it, a book talking directly to you. Well, it's your fault for showing an interest in how your country works.

From one Average American to another, I think you have what it takes.

In the summer of 2009 I was talking with a friend (online) about you and how we could possibly get you more involved. That is how committed I am to you being a part of the system. It seems that you are most likely a fine upstanding American who would love to get involved but often are unsure of how to do so. Well, following you will find the text from a website I created to take the initial guesswork out of our system. The name of the website is www.200Each.com and this is the best plan I can come up with to help get you more involved. And if not you, who? And if not now, when?

The following content comes directly from www.200Each.com: "Imagine a world in which our elected officials were the very best America had to offer, regardless of income level. Instead of boycotts and protests, voter drives and petitions, why not hit our elected officials where it really hurts, job security. As we all know, many of us are out of work or working jobs that we have to in order to get by. What if our elected officials worried about their jobs too?"

I am calling the idea "200 Each." The idea stems from the understanding that most of our elected officials seem to have forgotten who they work for. They know that they have at worst a fifty-fifty shot at staying in office because nobody else runs except, in most cases, the rival party's pick. Well, that part probably will not change, but imagine if within your own party you suddenly had to fight for the seat you've had for the last four years, and not against one, two, or three opponents, but one hundred. Imagine what you would think if one hundred people from your own party in your own district ran against you. We are betting that they would quickly start to care a bit more what the boss has to say about where things are headed.

In the meantime, you are watching, because on the other side of the debate for your job one hundred more people are fighting it out to be your opponent. This is a truly bipartisan plan of the people. We are the ones in charge and those on the Hill need to remember that. But it does not end there, a "100 Each" plan can be put in place for local state elections. All it takes is signatures to get your name on the ballot and we saw the confusion it caused with California in the governor's race a few years back.

Imagine the beauty of seeing the people of this country truly stand up by taking charge and using the constitutional powers guaranteed to us by the founding documents to literally take our country back and put it in the hands of the citizens. We don't have to change a single law to do this. It is an open contest so long as you pass the state and federal definitions of a lawful candidate.

Following, the Secretary of State websites for all fifty states are listed. In most states this is where you will need to start.

Once you have done that, contact your local city, county, or state party affiliated office to let them know you intend to run and expect their support. Republicans, Democrats, Libertarians, and Greens, all parties can do this. If you are interested in a federal seat, do the same on the federal level.

Good luck.
Alabama: http://www.sos.state.al.us/
Arizona: http://www.azsos.gov/
Arkansas: http://www.sos.arkansas.gov/
California: http://www.sos.ca.gov/
Colorado: http://www.sos.state.co.us/
Connecticut: http://www.ct.gov/sots/site/default.asp
Delaware: http://sos.delaware.gov/sos.shtml
Florida: http://election.dos.state.fl.us/
Georgia: http://www.sos.georgia.gov/
Idaho: http://www.sos.idaho.gov/
Illinois: http://www.cyberdriveillinois.com/
Indiana: http://www.in.gov/sos/
Iowa: http://www.sos.state.ia.us/
Kansas: http://www.kssos.org/
Kentucky: http://www.sos.ky.gov/
Louisiana: http://www.sos.louisiana.gov/
Maine: http://www.maine.gov/sos/
Maryland: http://www.sos.state.md.us/
Massachusetts: http://www.sec.state.ma.us/
Michigan: http://www.michigan.gov/sos
Minnesota: http://www.sos.state.ms.us/elections/elections.asp
Missouri: http://www.sos.mo.gov/
Montana: http://sos.mt.gov/
Nebraska: http://www.sos.ne.gov/dyindex.html
Nevada: http://sos.state.nv.us/
New Hampshire: http://www.sos.nh.gov/
New Jersey: http://www.state.nj.us/state/secretary/
New Mexico: http://www.sos.state.nm.us/
New York: http://www.dos.state.ny.us/

North Carolina: http://www.sosnc.com/
North Dakota: http://www.nd.gov/sos/
Ohio: http://www.sos.state.oh.us/
Oklahoma: http://www.sos.state.ok.us/
Oregon: http://www.sos.state.or.us/
Pennsylvania: http://www.sos.state.pa.us/
Rhode Island: http://www.state.ri.us/
South Carolina: http://www.scsos.com/
South Dakota: http://www.sdsos.gov/
Tennessee: http://www.tennessee.gov/sos/
Texas: http://texas.gov/sos/
Vermont: http://www.sec.state.vt.us/
Virginia: http://www.commonwealth.virginia.gov/
Washington: http://www.secstate.wa.gov/
West Virginia: http://www.wvsos.com/
Wisconsin: http://www.sos.state.wi.us/
Wyoming: http://soswy.state.wy.us/

The Lt. Governors of Alaska, Hawaii, and Utah are responsible for many of the functions usually associated with the Secretary of State.

Alaska: http://ltgov.state.ak.us/
Hawaii: http://hawaii.gov/ltgov
Utah: http://www.utah.gov/ltgovernor/

We have provided you with the tools to get started. From there it is up to the states to organize however you see fit to do so. But this is more of an individual effort, so run with it.

I will be contacting the office here in Nevada, so I only need 199 more people and Nevada is done. Imagine the news coverage of this if it picks up steam. Imagine the media having to report that thousands of people are running for hundreds of positions in the country, as they try to tell us what it means.

Are there not two hundred people in each district who care enough to run with this idea?

This is the very blueprint that should be used by any third party who really wants to have a meaningful showing in state elections. But more importantly, it is the blueprint for American citizen involvement.

A ways back I mentioned third-party people retaking the two major parties. Why is this idea important, you ask? It all has to do with infrastructure. In just about every town of any size in America you will find one of the following: a Democrat regional office or a GOP regional office. They are already set up to represent the geographic areas. All we need to do is remake them in our image.

In the old days the parties were easy to tell apart, and on some issue you can still find some very real differences, like abortion, taxation, military spending and support, etc. But, unfortunately, very few of those ideals translate over to actual application once these people are elected to office. Does the sheer altitude of elitism cause the rarified air around Washington DC to procreate dementia and deafness? Is it the intoxicating water of the Potomac? Something there has a profound effect on these people. It might be the power, who knows, but if they were not committed to being there long term, as most average Americans would not be, they might be more inclined to work at the job that they were hired to do and spend less time worrying about being reelected. Let's face it, when you are a working man or woman, you get reelected every day you go into work. You do a good job, the boss keeps you there; if you don't, you get bounced down the road. Perhaps the idea that one serves a limited term, and would come away with simple satisfaction rather than the benefits of royalty bestowed for life, would force some focus. That is the way the founders saw the situation. Nobody expected to make a life out of serving in Congress; in fact, all of the Founding Fathers had trades, professions, farms, or families they wanted to return to as quickly as they could do so.

This is the mentality that average Americans have about their day-to-day jobs, so why must we expect a non-lifetime politician to act any differently when they get to Congress or the presidency?  Do the job you were elected to do and if we like what we see, you get reelected. Remember this if you take nothing else away from this book, you are "term limits." Your vote decides who stays and who goes. There may be that rare man or woman who is immune to the Washington Plague and just works their butt off for the people and you might want to keep that person a bit longer than the others.

This could change things in every county, parish, and town across America. You will hear folks say that it won't change the money involved. I disagree. When you have two hundred candidates fighting it out for a seat in the Congress or one hundred fighting it out for the state house, the big money might sit on the sidelines until they have a better idea of which horse to bet on. No need to throw good money after bad by supporting the wrong person. In the meantime, real people get to put out an undiluted message from the heart based on real-world experiences; experiences some in Congress have never had to deal with. I would much rather see the guy who owns and operates a tractor dealing with the question of how to support small business than a Yale School of Law graduate. I would rather see a former pediatrician working on healthcare insurance reform with an insurance salesman than watch these folks in Washington DC rip a working system apart for the benefit of so few to the detriment of so, so many. I'm sorry, but a guy from ACORN does not have the real-life experience to tell a small-business owner how to make money and protect his assets. The best they can offer is how to get money from Uncle Sam and perhaps how to run a small illegal prostitution ring. (If this means nothing to you, Google "ACORN, prostitution, illegal teens, video" and learn what happened.)

And when that big money does enter the picture, it would sure be nice if the people running had collected enough in small donations to be able to turn it away. Imagine if big money couldn't get involved. Sure, they would throw it to someone else, but that alone would become a campaign issue, wouldn't it?

You now have the tools for change. You now know what needs to be changed, and most importantly, you now understand, at least to a better degree than you did before you sat down with this book, how these changes might affect you and how you are, in the end, the only one who can change anything.

# *Short Subject Essays*

## *The Reasons Why We Are Different ...*
## *Americans Compared to Others*

We live in a land created unlike any other nation on earth. From the first days of its inception it was based on a simple yet radical idea, that mankind was capable of self-governance. Not since the early days of Greece and Rome was the idea even entertained as most nations sprung up from the ashes of old ones.

In this country, however, we only had to break away from the shared history of all those European countries that now tremble at our feet and beg for our assistance. And this too is as it should be. We are the greatest nation to ever be founded with a purpose on the planet. We defend ourselves with a volunteer military, not one based on conscription and not one based on lower classes' servitude to their master's whims.

Our freedom in this country is based on the belief that it has always been here, mankind merely had to claim it as kings of their own domains. We Americans answer to a higher authority than any one man or king, and that is the law. Law governs our lives and those laws are passed by our elected representatives, not handed down from on high. From our founding this has been the understanding in this country; that no man, rich or poor, light or dark, elected or layman, educated or not, gay or straight, male or female, shall live above this sacred set of laws.

Our country grew out of strife, disgust with the way we kings were being treated by another king. We thought ourselves equal to this mere man across the Atlantic Ocean, who also put his pants on one leg at a time. Equals in nearly every way except one. We believed each other to be the same. We believed we were all of his majesty. Not one of us above another. It was this principle that later confronted us as a nation as we looked to the Black man with the same disdain that had once been leveled on mankind as a whole from those who wore crowns. So America did what it had to do at a cost of more than five hundred thousand lives to change America for the better. We fulfilled the full nature of our quest and made certain that all men were to be respected within our shores.

In later years as our freedom and liberty expanded our wealth to equal that of Europe as a whole, we were called upon to save the old country from itself as it ripped and tore at itself, one against another. While we chose sides, we did so based on those who would offer the most promise to the people still held in lesser positions by their leaders. And though our form of Republicanism never took root to the full extent it did here, we sat satisfied that we had done our level best to free the most we could. In the years that followed, more freedom was offered those people, and yet here, together we stood and took in millions more yearning to be truly free.

Still our wealth grew. Drawing on the strength of people from all over the world, free here like nowhere else to expand their gifts, be rewarded for their hard work, and be recognized for it with the full benefit of their ownership of it, whatever it was.

Are we perfect? No, far from it. But America and Americans represent the very best of what mankind can do when properly motivated with freedom to expand, to grow, and to accomplish.

And still our wealth grew, not just as individuals, but as a nation. Around the world we were recognized as the one place you could set your goals, no matter how high, and see them through. We split the atom, we reached the moon, and we did both in record time. But more than this, we made the small dreams of the individual reachable. It has been the accomplishment of all these otherwise minor dreams that have laid the foundation of this country. From the farmer in Iowa to the casino owners who pooled their money together to build a city in the desert that should not exist, the freedom to come together is what drives us as individuals.

But today that is threatened. It would be unwise to assume that the cause is some major world-changing event like terrorism, Communism, or even liberalism, although all have left their unmistakable mark on the foundation of this country. No, I say there are two major strains on this country today, either of which if allowed to expand could doom it.

First is the lowly hyphen. Yes, a simple, otherwise nondescript little keyboard-generated line a centimeter long, yet with it comes the power to change a country as mighty as the United States of America. From where does this insignificant little, oftentimes misused, former back bench shift only accessible IBM roller bar add-on find the power to bring down a nation? The answer is simple: from its use as a wall.

In days of old, people would come to America to be American. They would dare the seas to stop them in the belly of great ships and on the waves in small rafts, spitting into the wind in defiance just to step foot on a land only read about in books that had avoided the fire. Once on American soil you could see them shed the shackles of their former homes and embrace, for all its gold and glitz, modern problems and growing pains, the possibility of a better life. America made only one promise, opportunity. And that was all they needed.

Immigrants from the four corners of the earth, from China, Egypt, Serbia, Brazil, Soviet Russia, Israel, Korea, South Africa, Iran, Cuba, and every other country that can be named, they came forth promising only one thing in return, to be good Americans.

And they fulfilled that promise in ways and with stories only they will ever truly know. They became Americans in every way possible. Retaining their cultures they made America's richer by sharing their very best qualities.

Today, the hyphen threatens that stability, that cohesion that once made being American such an incredible moniker to behold. "African-American, Hispanic-American, Irish-American, Gay-American," and so on, and so on, creates divisions within the once great melting pot that was America. I for one refuse to recognize the power the hyphen holds, but for so many it becomes the first stick poking through the fence and later a wall in itself. Sadly, most who use it have no claim on it at all as they are born and bred Americans.

"A house divided cannot stand" goes the adage. And here today we see the bricks falling free and the people losing their once assimilated culture, and locking back on those shackles thrown off just a few generations ago.

In my youth I knew many people who traced their lineage to other countries. The O'sheas, the Stallonis, even a family with the last name Chin. And though we all knew the countries of origin of the names, we thought nothing of it as we all shared a common American heritage. I never introduced a friend by description, "This is my Italian-American friend, Tony." It never crossed our minds. He was just Tony.

Pride in the country your forefather came from is great; the heritage those people brought with them is wonderful. But remember, they brought it with them when they made the conscious decision to leave that country. Remember that, for all its culture, for all its conceived superiority today, they left it with the fullest of intention by most to never return to it or to see their children be a part of it. A better life, they believed, could only be found here, in America. Being part of a greater plan, a larger picture, and enjoying an open invitation for successfully achieving, that was their legacy to you, far more than the impression your name may imply.

The second thing that threatens to devour our nation is dependence; dependence on government to provide when your opportunity is thought to be unobtainable. Can you imagine General Washington at Valley Forge rallying his men with words like, "Tonight we cross icy death for healthcare reform," or President Lincoln at Gettysburg reminding the audience, "Four score and seven years ago, our forefathers came forth to ensure that the most successful among us would be taxed at a 70 percent income tax rate"? Of course not. Yet today the created need, and that is what it has been, perpetrated by Left and Right, Democrat and Republican, over the many decades since the turn of the last century, is what is offered constantly by government to those suffering from their own broken illusions.

Creating the problem and then continuing to expand it has ensured only one thing: a vote in November. The worst part of it all is that those who picked up those shackles and placed them on their legs most often did it out of self-defeat, not desire. Today, generation upon generation of those in shackles have bred into this subculture (often the same who most prominently use the hyphen mentioned earlier), and have produced the very same results for their descendants that those brave travelers fought so hard to leave: despair.

Regardless of these twin pillars of destruction, America still holds the promise it once did. Oh, I admit it is a bit rusty as less and less Americans use it and it retains little of its initial luster as so many have failed to pass to the next generation a love of country and fellow patriots. Yet while those in despair toil away at building this wall of exclusion higher, many more are coming to recognize the power these two simple yet powerful things are exercising on our great country. Those who still believe in the promise of opportunity are making themselves heard.

Recently, a book was written by Craig Ferguson, the host of *The Late Late Show* on CBS. In January of 2008 he became an American citizen and scored 100 percent on his American citizenship test. The title of his book is quite telling in this day and age that there are still those who believe in opportunity. It is called *American by Choice*. It is sad that a new American citizen had to remind many of us of the hard choices made by most of our forefathers. It is telling that the future may yet hold the brightest of futures for such a young country that calls its own flag Old Glory....

But what would I know; I'm just an Average American.

## What? Why? How? Huh? Who?

(Originally posted on VoiceofArizona.com on February 9, 2009. At the time this was posted it was argued that total deficit spending would not exceed $750 billion for the fiscal year.)

I have a few simple questions that I am hoping the Left can explain to me in simple terms. Why is $1.5 trillion of deficit spending by Obama acceptable but the deficit spending by Reagan and Bush was not?

And why has the economy not shot up like a rocket at the very notion of all this money hitting the system? And why has the market dropped more than sixteen hundred points since Obama was elected when all we need was some change to make it all right? And why is Pelosi acting like the chief executive and why is Obama allowing it?

Why are you allowing the idea of capping corporate CEO income for those who take federal money when you know that soon enough (in fact, Barney Frank has already started writing the legislation) they will want to cap all income for corporate executives whether their company is making money or not? How long do you suspect it will be until they tell you that you make too much money because your company is failing in some way?

Why have we not seriously looked at a tax holiday for all to infuse money back into the market and economy? It would cost the federal government nothing to do if they simply said that for the next (fill in the blank for amount of time) we are not going to take money from you, so use it on what you need to save your company, balance your personal budgets, or invest in your company's need for new machinery or infrastructure, and in the meantime we in government are going to cut the fat out of our spending to compensate for the shortfall in revenue for the same (fill in the blank) time period.

And where exactly in the Constitution does the government have the power to take over and run private entities anyway? Will you expect them to do a better job than they did with Fannie Mae and Freddie Mac? And in what enterprise run by the government do you see the pattern success that you feel will carry over into this new role as commander in chief executive of all failing companies?

Why have we not looked seriously at cutting the corporate tax rates on foreign companies that wish to do business in this county as a means to entice them to invest billions in our economy instead of borrowing it from other countries who may one day call in those marks?

Is everything not on the table regarding our economy like it is with the War on Terror?

And again I want to ask the question: How can our government spend more than it brings in? Why can it do it when I can't? Why do we not look at Uncle Sam as a failure when he has to borrow trillions but we sure do corporations whose economic outlook has suddenly shifted when we have watched the Feds do this for the better half of a century?

To those of you who say the government takes on a fatherlike role in running the country, I say that the behavior of these companies is a learned trait after watching the government run things into the ground for so long, run massive deficits, and turn to the people for help; they figure if it's good enough for the goose ... And I will say that I believe those of you supporting the idea of allowing the government to now strap your children with another $1.5 trillion in debt are hypocrites, when just three months ago that was one of Bush's biggest faults.

Obviously, you have had some change of heart or the Kool-Aid Obama hands out is tainted with crack for you to be so ignorant.

Give me real answers to these questions because I want to understand why it is okay now but it wasn't then.

But what would I know; I'm just an Average American.

# Greed: The Basic Building Block of Societal Expansion

(Originally posted December 28, 2008 at VoiceofArizona.com.)

We all remember the movie *Wall Street* with Michael Douglas as Gordon Gekko, the stereotypical Wall Street robber baron, and that famous line, "Greed is good." But how many of you really took that to heart? How many of you saw that and thought to yourself, "Typical Republican, always out for themselves"?

I'm sure many of you, based on the things you have written here, were quite impressed with this not so died-in-the-wool caricature of the mean and ruthless, in your eyes "Reagan-like," self-centered, all for one and one for one 1980s Republican. But in his words was a world a truth. For it is greed that has moved this country, and for that matter this animal called man, forward by leaps and bounds instead of baby steps.

In the last one hundred years we have witnessed the birth of most of the great business models operating on the planet today. Think back to life before the telephone, the computer, the car, plane, modern grocery stores with refrigeration. Commerce, my friends, is the purest form of greed and the most virtuous.

Do you like diamonds, ladies? Greed brings them out of the ground. Do you like to drink beer and wine, eat cheese with your doctor and lawyer friends while driving back and forth to your "holiday parties" in your imported Japanese and German or English automobiles? Greed brings it all to you. Perhaps you like the idea of being able to hear your baby from another room, or vaccinate him or her from the deadly diseases of the world. Greed created them, ships them, warehouses them, and pays for the research and development of them. Nothing on this planet happens without a sufficient profit motive. And nothing should. I give you the Roman Catholic Church and the Latter-day Saints (Mormons) as two examples of organizations whose entire focus is good works, yet there is an incredible profit motive at work here and has been in the case of the Catholics for nearly two thousand years. But look how the LDS have worked to catch up. Oh, heaven's going to be a crowded place!

The Utopians among us will argue that some people do the right things for the right reasons and they will have a point. But "some" is not most. How many of them donate 100 percent of the money made from those products to the people who buy them? And how many of them are so convinced that the government is the best steward of their wealth and treasury that they give above and beyond their tax liability to the government to help finance those very important programs that they constantly defend day in and day out? I'll give you a second to think that one over. You hear Warren Buffett talk of a heavy tax burden for guys like him. Well that's great, but does he write a bigger check than the law requires at the end of the year? No, he doesn't. Instead he gives away billions to his and other charitable organizations because he must think they do a better job with the money. No, he does it because of the profit associated with being Warren Buffett. Advertising his good works is part of his job.

Greed is what drives most of us to work every day. Deny it if you want, but you're only producing the smoke and mirrors for yourself. We know from world history, CNN, the Children's Christian Feed the Starving Little African programs that most of the world survives on little. So don't come back and tell me that you work to support your family, put a roof over their head, and place food on your table. You can do that for $500 a month in many parts of this country. Live in a shack, eat what you kill, and you have the necessities of this life covered. But that's not what you want, is it?

Hell no, it isn't! At least I am honest enough to say I want a big-ass house, of which I own a couple, a big-ass car, of which I own a few, and a big-ass bank account, which I now have, so that I can do what I want when I want to do it. That big-ass car has hauled more turkey dinners this year than ever before, and the big-ass bank account funded it. My greed paid for the home builder to build my houses, putting dozens of people to work. Detroit should kiss my ass for all the American steel I have floating around this planet right now, hundreds more workers there would offer up a thank-you if the Union would allow them to think for themselves. And every time I take a vacation to yet another great American city I am spreading the wealth with my fellow citizens who only so gleefully take it right out of my hot little hand. You know why? Because they're greedy, too, and God bless them for it.

So the next time any of you want to sit in your ivory towers and look down your noses at me and my ilk, feel free to offer up your holdings to the first person who asks, because you are not greedy. Go ahead and write check for twice what Uncle Sam says you have to pay them, just post it here so we can see that you are the real enlightened one, and not a poser like the rest of the liberals in this country who talk a good game but have little commitment to really get their hands dirty. People like me live our philosophy every day. Shouldn't you live yours?

And over $600,000,000 (Obama's campaign war chest) tells me that liberals have it in them; they are willing to pay for the right to get all their stuff free from others, which is the worst form of greed. My greed makes me work hard to help others through commerce, but your greed makes you do nothing and expect everyone else to work hard to take care of you, thus enslaving not only yourself but all those who have to work harder to take up your slack. Liberating and freedom inspiring is the way America used to be before the advent of the modern American liberal.

Our world has been moved forward by greed. Every step of the way!

But what would I know; I'm just an Average American.

## Those Who Do Not Learn from History . . .

(Originally posted November 2, 2008 on VoiceofArizona.com.)
We have all heard the old saying "Those who do not learn from history are doomed to repeat it." This year we are being

force-fed by most media the idea that we are witnessing history in the making and that if there is any repeating of history at work here, it is to be the 1980 Reagan Revolution that we are watching in modern times and geared toward Progressive thought. An awakening of sorts to the supposed failures of the aforementioned 1980s scenario.

Of course, that can only be seen in hindsight and we are nowhere near the point of judging the current presidency let alone the last one. Some of you may be gasping at that statement but look back at the last really hated Republican to leave office, Richard Nixon. For decades Nixon was held over the heads of GOP runners as the poster child of what not be, whom not to sound like, and whom not to resemble in any way, shape, or form. Yet today, through the lenses of history, Nixon's presidency is seen for what it was: a great success internationally and even here at home. I mean, you have to remember this is the man who ended Vietnam. The most hated war America has ever engaged in, at least until recent events.

But history can offer us a way to focus on things that are likely to come in the future, although there can be no guarantees. Take Jimmy Carter, for example. Two terms in the House and a full term as governor of an average-size state. Most indications were that he would be an average to better than average president, plus, he didn't have any of the Nixon stink on him like Ford did.

Ronald Reagan, former two-term governor of a state that if broken away from the US would yield between the seventh and tenth largest economy in the world and about the fourth largest military on earth (during the 1980s when more bases were still open). But he was an actor so many thought we would get little in the way of real change and instead be fed a lot of lip service. They were certainly off on that one.

Bill Clinton, on his fourth term as governor of a poor state, went on to actually do very little damage to this country save for making us look weak around the world, allowing for major deregulation of the banking industry, and the occasional Oval Office perversion. Other than that he did a great job.

Today we are faced with the very real possibility (and that's all it is, a possibility) that Obama, a two-month senator (because that's when he started running for president) with a long background as a community organizer (funny) who has not written a single piece of legislation providing for any hope or change, but who did find time to write two books about himself, is seriously being considered by some voters as "The One" to move this country forward. (Long sentence I know, thanks for hanging in there with me.)

Let's look at this situation through history and see if we can try to put a bead on which former presidency Mr. Obama's orgasmically dreamed of election would hold for his supporters.

His supporters want you to think Reagan-like Revolution, leading to thirty-plus years of Democratic control of Capitol Hill with Democrats taking the White House in three of four elections to follow. A planetary change in how America is perceived around the world and a reawakening of America as the leader of the free world and a financial giant who cannot be ignored. These were indeed the outcomes of Reagan's presidency, but Obama is no Ronald Reagan. When Reagan spoke he told us of a new dawn, a shining city on a hill, and of the good and strength of the American people. Obama tells us of how bad we have it now and that only government can solve our problems, problems, by the way, that most of us are not experiencing at the moment.

Another look at the cycle leads one to see Obama not as the next Reagan or a Democrat version of him, instead it points to him winning by default due to people's dislike for the current party in office. Let's look at another time this happened and how it all panned out.

Reagan ran for election during this very same cycle, and, unfortunately for him, his day was not yet at hand. The year was not 1980, but 1976. A Republican was in office that had done an okay job but was stained by the one act only he could perform: the pardoning of Richard Millhouse Nixon, perhaps the most hated politician in American history to date.

Gerald Ford was tainted b having been Nixon's VP and was essentially thrown out with the bathwater. What replaced him was a seasoned politician with a long background of service to this nation as representative, a governor, and navy submariner. He was even a small-business owner growing peanuts. A fine enough resume for any president past or present.

Once in office he too had a dream of government taking the lead in providing for the people. He gave us a Secretary of Education to ensure that education remained a top priority in this country and a Secretary of Energy. (Sidebar—has anyone mentioned lately how great the education system in this country is or how low priced energy is and how thankful we are that we have abundant supplies here at home? Good thing these two seats were added to the table, they proved to be complete wastes of time and money judging from the results. Education has slid into the toilet and all the Department of Energy has managed to do is make it hard for energy to be developed at home.) Anyway, he also had little backbone and our enemies knew it. Iran took hostages 444 days prior to the end of his term as president and Carter's reaction was to throw broken helicopters at them, having gutted the military. And lest we forget the dangers of acid rain, the environmental movement in this country got a major foothold under this fine upstanding man. He thought it a good idea to make the arrangements to turn over control of the Panama Canal, a vital lifeline for commerce for the United States, to Panama, who in turn hired the Chinese to run things for them, essentially putting China in a position of power over a portion of our commerce worldwide. And then there was the massive growth in personal wealth America enjoyed under his leadership. Oh, wait, that's not right, is it? Sorry, had to fact-check this one real quick. Interest rates at 22 percent, 8 percent unemployment, incredible inflationary pressures, high gas prices because of an oil embargo, and … it goes on and on and on. Pick it and you will see the Carter administration's fingerprints on it.

And don't forget this guy had a solid resume. I mean it! Obama does not have such a resume.

Now fast-forward to 2008. We have a hated president in office, we are in two regional wars (don't forget, the Left turned on Nixon even after he ended the war in Vietnam, they wasted no time throwing him under the bus even when he gave them what they wanted), there is a generalized belief by many that change is what is needed, as in 1976, and so long as it looks different, acts different, and sounds different, it must be good. Well, Carter was an agent of change and he changed us a bunch.

Those who do not learn from history are doomed to repeat it. We are repeating it, folks, and the good news is that *if* Obama pulls a win out over McCain, which I still don't think is a lock especially considering Obama's internals that tell him 10 percent of his numbers are made up, but *if* Obama wins this thing, we most likely have only one term to live through before the return of sanity. The real question for those of us in the Conservative Movement is more direct and pressing. Who's the next Reagan? Romney had a failed run this year as Reagan did in 1976. So did Huckabee. Do we have a plan if we get another Carter? Think about it, folks. It matters.

But what would I know; I'm just an Average American.

(Update: It scares me to think how dead-on I was back then.)

## What Is It Going to Take?

(Originally posted June 9, 2008, on VoiceofArizona.com.)

This started as a comment on another article. The debate about financing of a party for delegates from the state already in trouble financially was the primary focus. It got me thinking, I have not heard much about Louisiana in the past months except for New Orleans. I thought to myself, "What about the rest of the state, what's going on there? Who the hell is running that train wreck?" So I did a little research ... Here are my feelings and the results of what I found and why I believe Louisiana could well be starting to become the model for conservatism in the future, which is simply a return to the proven results rooted in conservatism.

You know the real question is: "Why do the people of New Orleans continue to suffer?" At this point it appears to be self-inflicted to some degree.

In America we have the freedom and right to relocate any time we desire a change. If you live in an area that is crime ridden, you can move away from it. This applies equally to those who live in an area that has been devastated by some natural disaster.

Look at the people in Kansas. A small town there was absolutely razed in the fashion of Genghis Khan (a Kerry replay) by a tornado. It has been more than a year since this happened. The town is well on its way to being rebuilt and with all new technology. See http://www.usatoday.com/news/nation/2008-05-01-greensburg_N.htm.

These people have taken what the planet threw at them and did so without blaming anyone. They have turned everything around. New Orleans still wallows in both filth and self-pity. True, there are some areas that are rebuilding and trying to move forward, but for the most part the city is a bruise on the American way of life.

New Orleans is a symptom of a much larger problem in the United States. They represent the "give me" state mentality that conservatism stands so adamantly against. In the weeks after the levies broke, levies run by both the Corps of Engineers and the local city, county, and state government, mind you, things did not go smoothly. I realize this. But in the months, and then years, that followed it has become apparent that a large portion of the city has little intention of doing what is necessary to come out of the situation stronger than they entered it.

"Somebody do for me" seems to permeate the mentality of locals. Where is the dominating American spirit of overcoming adversity, of rising to meet the challenges that lay before us, of doing for oneself?

What message is sent to the children of this country as they see a predominantly Black (or "Chocolate," to quote their mayor) city continue to suffer seemingly for the sake of suffering? They have the ability to rise above this situation but it almost appears that they don't for some political gain.

Well, they have a new governor now. Bobby Jindal is a driving, youthful, forward-looking, thirty-six-year-old Republican who is forcing the state to become fiscally responsible. In addition, he is encouraging the people to prepare for another hurricane that could very well strike. Through ethics reform in a state that has been poorly run for decades and reducing those taxes that have stood in the way of progress, he has energized the state and taken the lead in just about every aspect of how the state is now run. Now he has turned his attention, having built a solid foundation for forward movement, to the people themselves. The state's workforce development program, long since hailed as poorly run and corrupt, is being revamped and rebuilt from the ground up. Today, ninety-five thousand jobs are available in Louisiana, 55 percent of those requiring nothing more than a high school diploma, 35 percent requiring an associate's degree or two-year certification of training in the desired field, and 10 percent needing a four-year degree or higher. These are core jobs, bread-and-butter employment for many of the state's poor and lower middle class. These are the jobs that can lift them out of the current situation. Why are they not clamoring to take them and start repairing their miserable lives? This is primarily because the education system in Louisiana has turned out crap education by not preparing these people for the workforce over the last twenty years. Jindal could tout, as we have seen hundreds of time on the Left, some platitude about the children.... Remember the children.... Well, he knows about the children but not to the detriment of the people who are responsible for the children, the parents. Oh, he's working on changing the education in the state, too, but the major focus right now is getting the parents back to work.

Instead of increasing Welfare payments and child lunch programs, he has taken the long-range view of preparing the people to not need them ... The audacity of long-range thinking.

Here is the future of Louisiana, conservatism, the Republican Party, and America itself.

But what would I know; I'm just an Average American.

(Update: Have you seen the way Bobby Jindal has stepped out in front of the world on the BP oil spill? Can I call a leader or what?)

# *Crying Wolf*

(Originally posted November 5, 2007.)

Naomi Wolf: the literary genius who brought us such great works of art as *The Beauty Myth* (1991) in which she lamented the poor girls who want to look pretty. Her five areas where women were under attack: work, religion, sex, violence, and hunger.

Human nature says ugly girls don't get ahead in the workplace, in their religions (I guess it is the second-fiddle thing that most churches in America have thrown out), in sex (yep, it's always rape), violence (nobody should be beaten unless they are terrorist trying to kill you), and hunger. Hunger? What the hell? Get a burger.

She followed up with zinger after zinger of a little salt. "Wolf's later books are *Fire with Fire* (1993) on politics, female empowerment and women's sexual liberation, *Promiscuities* (1997) on adolescence and female sexuality, and *Misconceptions* (2001) on childbirth" (Wikipedia). Wow, like women have not given birth for a few generations prior to her sudden revelations.

This is the same woman who claimed that 150,000 women die of anorexia each year when the actual number is closer to one hundred and was an Al Gore advisor on getting the female vote. That worked out well, didn't it?

So with a long list of debunked theories and misadventures into the man's world that she just can't understand (although women from Margaret Thatcher to Madonna have thrived in it regardless of the supposed rules) she now wants us to believe that her intense research has shown her the ten steps leading to fascism:

1. Invoke a terrifying internal and external enemy. You mean when we were actually attacked on 9/11?
2. Create a gulag. You mean the prisons being built partly because of overpopulated prisons in this country?
3. Develop a thug caste. Muslims, regardless of where they were from, attacked us.

4. Set up an internal surveillance system. Aye, I hate those freeway cameras.
5. Harass citizens' groups. Like this has not been going on for generations in this country from the NAACP to the KKK.
6. Engage in arbitrary detention and release. You mean of those shooting guns at our guys in a foreign war? Get real.
7. Target key individuals. This must be the Code Pink people.
8. Control the press. The same press that bashes Bush at every turn and makes him out to be an even bigger idiot than he might be?
9. Dissent equals treason. This is paranoia at work.
10. Suspend the rule of law. Hasn't happened yet, and there are 435 other people on Capitol Hill who covet their power too much to hand it over like this suggests.

I read this in its original version from the *Guardian* in England. If she has revised any of it for her new book of the same title, forgive me. I have no interest in feeding this beast with my hard-earned income.

At first glance it seems logical. These things would have to be in place for a fascist regime to rise up and take control of a country. The list contains some obvious prerequisites for an overthrow from having a private army (read Blackwater) to surveillance (think Patriot Act) to the gulag (read Blackwater and Halliburton building prisons in the desert). Yep, she's got them all, except the most obvious ones. The *whys*.

She compares much of what Bush has been supposedly doing to Hitler, Mussolini, and Stalin. But she misses the reasons these men did what they did. First up, they wanted to be part of the elite class. All were relatively low on the class totem pole in their respective countries. Hitler was an illegitimate poor bastard who lived on an orphan's pension and was previously beaten by his father. A real rising star in the German republic, wasn't he? Mussolini was born poor as dirt to a teacher and a blacksmith. He was kicked out of schools for fighting and deported from Switzerland in his early years. The guy was no Rockefeller. And

Stalin, he was another poor bastard beaten by his drunken dad. No fast track to power here.

These kinds of upbringings also apply to Castro, who, though born into some money, was raised in foster homes.

Bush, on the other hand, is a child of privilege. Where is his motivation for power and control over a world that has treated him unfairly? It isn't there. Nor is it in Cheney's background. This man needs nothing from us as he has plenty of money at his disposal and is one of the upper class. (Update: Her theories may well apply to Obama, however.)

Also not in her deep digging into history does she mention that each and every one of these countries had toyed with dictatorship to one degree or another whether by monarchy or formerly failed attempts for single leadership many times in the past. In America we are well aware of the history of these other countries and can clearly assess what is an attempt to free the hands of a president who is charged with the duty of protecting us from foreign invasion (attack, I think, is covered there as well, although not particularly mentioned) and the beginnings of an end to our freedom.

I can also see where, when one has a premise and is trying to prove it, one can easily connect the dots in retrospect. Much as the supporters of Christ and every generation since the death of Christ have been able to point to events in their lifetime and conclude that his return is right around the corner. Of course, Christ made it clear that we would not know the date or the time, but it is human nature to speculate.

These ten signs of the coming collapse of our system of government are just that, signs of an impending fascist regime more likely envisioned in the mind of the writer based on a fear she carries than in any concrete facts on the ground or in the minds of leaders today. (Update: At least until Obama showed up on the scene.) She even forgot the part where the pending takeover is supported in large part by the elimination of arms from the populous. (Update: Also on Obama's list of things to do this year or next, through the UN no less.)

It is Australia, not America, who should be careful. ... They lost their guns a few years ago.

No, this is just another attempt at fearmongering from another Left-leaning Bush hater. Though touted as some marvelous piece of literature, I doubt it will sell as good as her book on Woman Power did, except in those arenas like Randi Rhoads and Tom Hartman who have latched on to Naomi and are doing their best to spread this ridiculous tripe.

But what would I know; I'm just an Average American.

## The Melting Pot Is Rusting

(Originally posted September 3, 2007, on VoiceofArizona.com.)

Do any of you remember what we learned in school, back before public education in America was, and I paraphrase here, such as, and the Iraq, South African, it should be for the future, and such as for the Asians? (If this doesn't make sense to you, go to youtube.com and search Miss Teen America, South Carolina.)

Back when I was in grade school the march toward equality of outcome in education had already started. Although I did not realize it at the time, those who were having problems in class were holding the rest of us back; therefore, the equality of outcome was based on the lowest common denominator instead of the highest possible obtainable expectation. Perhaps this is part of the problem with America today.

In recent years I have been lucky enough to come in contact with a huge number of people who are activists in the purest sense of the word. They are actively trying to change America. I have met them on both sides of the aisle, holding just about every viewpoint you can have on damn near any subject you want to present. Not all of these issues are of interest to me, but I listen and/or read and lend a hand where I think I might do some good. This brings us to the latest issue that has hit the radar screen locally.

It has not hit with a pounding thud, but with a small foot soldier's constant march. Little by little American business is beginning to accept one very important variation on the way things have always been done in this country: They are beginning to conduct and actively seek revenue from people who cannot or simply do not choose to speak or read our language.

I was disappointed that this country, which has been predominantly English speaking for the better part of the last two hundred years, has allowed for Spanish radio and Spanish television to be produced and broadcast over the public airwaves, but I accepted it as something about which there was little anyone could do. I'm sure by now we have Arabic-language radio and TV along with a number of others, and I can only hope that the messages coming from these stations are of a benevolent thread and not a call to arms. I was then further disappointed when local government started wasting taxpayer dollars on printing bilingual ballots for our elections. Termed at the time as a way to get more voters involved, it was thought that by doing this more naturalized Americans would get involved in the body politic and take a greater role of exercising their rights in their new homeland. ACLU forbid we expect them to do what every other group of immigrants has done in this country and actually learn the language in order to feel more a part of this new land.

Then a few years ago I noticed the junk mail that I receive started being printed in both English and Spanish. This just irritated me but I thought, well, if a company wants to spend its revenue on something to gain more business from a part of the nation it might otherwise not be getting, that's their right to do so. It's not public funds they are spending so who am I to tell them what to do with their profits. This, of course, reached a head with the multicultural Yellow Pages, which I believe Quest puts out. I also determined at that time that I would personally no longer do business with any company that panders to the non-English-speaking minority of this country as it is my right to decide who I do business with. I only wish I could decide what taxes to pay based on this same test.

Since then I have watched the once immense list of American companies I would be proud to do business with shrink. I am a Chevy man. My Tahoe is one of my self-serving, needless, gas-guzzling, environmentally reprehensible, Republican status symbols that I enjoy most of all, but GM now has Spanish billboards in this town promoting their new 2008 lineup of cars. Ford lost me with the Festiva (it's a joke—like I was ever going to drive a car that small and fuel efficient). Wal-Mart, JCPenney's, Mervyn's, and just about every other major and minor retail store now panders as well, as does damn near every business I go into. The computer I am using right now is built by HP and I noticed after I bought it that the operating and installation instructions were in Spanish on the back side. And I'm sure Microsoft has left the reservation, too. Hell, two of the most listened to country music songs last year were about a Mexican girl by George Strait and Kenny Chesney's little number about living in Mexico. So what's a red-blooded American supposed to do?

Find peace in the one American institution that still stands for the English-speaking American, the National Rifle Association, the good ole NRA. WRONGO!!!!!

Allow me to share a short tale from a friend …

The NRA recently endorsed our fine upstanding Sanctuary City creating Mayor Phil (just let them come on in) Gordon (mayor of Phoenix, Arizona, at the time). They posted this on their website, both the English and *Spanish* sides of it. When some of my informed friends called the NRA to ask them why they would endorse a man whose views on immigration were so wrongheaded, they were informed, and I quote, "The NRA doesn't look at immigration as an issue; the only thing the NRA looks at is a stand on the 2nd Amendment." The NRA representative went on to explain that a large number of gun owners in the US are Spanish speaking. As my friend said, "That's just fine, and they can speak Spanish at home ... but if they are *Americans*, and even if they were naturalized, they should be speaking English and the NRA needs to stop pandering."

The conversation at that point was essentially over. The NRA representative told my friend that endorsements were under the control of the NRA's California organization (which may help explain the stupidity of it all) and to call there if she didn't agree. Instead she told them what her plan was, which included not re-upping her membership next year.

What else do we have to lose for those coming here to feel included? Should I change my name to Premedio Americano, or Americano de Premedio? They came here to join this country, not the other way around. If we go there or anywhere in this world we have to adjust our lifestyle to the local culture's lifestyle.

It makes me sick. … Melting Pot, not anymore. Today we have a short-order grill where you can order up the America that makes you most comfortable à la carte.... Assimilation is futile.

But what would I know; I'm just a Premedio Americano.

(Update: I have fully changed my mind since then about Ford Motor Company. Being the only automaker in the US to not take federal money I now fully endorse them and their products. Just keep the profits coming, boys.)

## Have Unions Outlived Their Usefulness?

(Originally posted October 28, 2005, on VoiceofArizona.com.)

The question is simple. The answer not so much. Early in the history of this country the question of child labor, workplace safety, and employee benefits were a take it or leave it proposal. Children were not allowed to work in harsh conditions; they were often forced to do so. Workplace safety was managed by simply hiring a replacement for the guy killed in the mine, buried in the concrete on a dam construction site, or pulled into the machinery that manufactured your goods. And as for benefits, they were the sole province of the upper class, the management and corporate types.

Then entered the idea of collective bargaining. Have the workers stand with one voice and threaten to walk off the job if certain demands were not met, if children were not protected, safety not addressed, and benefits not provided to show a sort of appreciation for the worker staying with a company for many years or even a lifetime. All noble ideas.

Turn to the current day and look at General Motors, Ford, and Chrysler. The first two are still American companies; Chrysler is being absorbed by Daimler. They all have entered into collective bargaining agreements over the years that have in many ways stifled their ability to compete on the world market. GM alone has a "benefit budget" that is bigger than its manufacturing, marketing, and transportation budgets combined. People yell and scream that the CEO compensation packages and governmental regulations have in part led to this problem. But the real problem here has been the unions. They have forced, through the threat of strike, a major portion of our economic machine to kneel before them and be placed in a kind of corporate "time-out." Don't get me wrong, GM and Ford and others agreed to these requirements instead of letting the workforce walk like Caterpillar did in the 1990s (only to have the union accept the original proposal put forth by management years earlier, and during which the white-collar guys took to the production floor only to increase production and quality until the strike ended).

Today we have laws prohibiting child labor in dangerous environments, wages at most places that are nonunion have stayed competitive (for which we might have unions to thank, I admit the possibility), and benefits are now commonplace. The point is unions have caused as much bad as good. The mentality that the "company" will take care of you in your old age has led many to not prepare for the future on their own. If the company goes broke now, they are in trouble, i.e., United Airlines. And let's not forget OSHA and ANSI, both government bodies who live, eat, and breathe safety regulation.

I'm not a union basher, but I think the time may have come to seriously consider the end of organized labor as it exists today. The world is not the breadlines of the early 1930s, the world market is no longer the town, county, state, or even country we live in, it is truly the world. Business needs to be able to compete. Outsourcing, another probable side effect of union wages and benefits rising, is the natural reaction of a company trying to stay alive and profitable.

Many companies have moved from pension plans solely financed by the company to 401(k)s, generally regarded as good for the company and the worker. Workers have some control over where the money goes to grow, and, thanks to Reagan, it is no longer considered part of the corporate assets and cannot be touched by the company for any reason, thus ensuring it will be there when retirement comes around. We all know that Social Security won't be there for us in the future (news flash if you were not aware of this).

Lastly, when did profit become a four-letter word? Note to union leaders nationwide: When the profit is all used up giving you all the benefits and wages you want, the company goes under. I know that should I ever exercise my freedom to start a small business, *profit* will be a good thing.

One more thought, could it be that the unions know this already? Maybe it is just the idea that within the Democratic Party they still hold some power. Power, like profit, can be a driving force for someone on the verge of irrelevance.

## Never Forget

(Originally posted November 11, 2005, on VoiceofArizona.com.)

Once a year we stand together and say thank-you to those men and women who have offered up the ultimate sacrifice for us. These brave men and women don't do it for glory, land, or to spread our way of life, most do it simply to defend their own family, secure a future for their children, and to preserve their own freedom to have a good life in a free country.

People like me, who choose not to serve, owe these individuals an enormous thank-you on Veterans Day and every day that we benefit from their courageous actions. Too often they are forgotten in the hustle and bustle of everyday life. Sure, right now when there is a war going on we tend to make mention to them that we appreciate what they did, but what about in peacetime? They deserve it even more then.

The next time you are at a family BBQ and you know that a family member or friend served, tell them you are thankful, and tell others who might not know what they did for their country. In reality it is really the only thing we can do and most of all it is all they would ever want us to do.

My father is a veteran of the Korean War (I say war, the Pentagon still says police action, and my dad says war—he was there, he should know), a proud marine, and I make sure each and every Veterans Day that I take the time to let him know that what he did for his children and grandchildren is not being squandered by us. I also call my best friend from high school who was also a marine in the first Gulf War. And finally I call my cousin, a former Vietnam navy pilot and recent retiree from United Airlines. Each of these calls meant the world to these three very different veterans. Each sincerely thanked me for remembering them on this day.

That is really the point to all this. I know I am usually on here opining over some liberal cause I can't stand or talking up the beliefs I hold as a Republican Party member, but today is different. Today I make a promise to all those veterans out there regardless of political slant, creed, color, religious belief, or economic situation: I WILL NEVER FORGET.

I will never forget what you did for me, my wife to be, and my kids. I will never forget the sacrifices of my grandfather, my many uncles, cousins, and friends who have served stateside or overseas, those who saw action like my father or those who did not like a friend of mine who served all four years in Idaho. Or those men and women who served as nurses and doctors in combat zones.

We are a diverse nation of people, all with a common goal, to live free. These are the people who were given that gift in their youth and kept it to give to us. So I say once more, you are remembered, appreciated, and respected. And to those of you who are going to serve in the future, you are walking in the shoes of giants—giants like my dad. I thank you in advance.

On this Veterans Day take a minute; thank a Vet and NEVER EVER FORGET!

# *Divorce: One Cause of America's Pain*

(Originally posted November 21, 2005, on VoiceofArizona.com.)

I read an article about education on this site and I must admit it is indeed in a serious state of disarray. I often wonder what is the real problem, the "root" cause of all the problems we face as we embark on the twenty-first century. Crime, housing, Welfare, the poor, children not behaving, and such can all be linked to one choice people make in this country: divorce.

In the last fifty years divorce has become something people do almost as often as they change their underwear. We see it every day playing out on the TV, the movies, and, unfortunately, our bedrooms. Out with the old, in with the new.

My fiancée and I were talking about the situation earlier today (both of us divorced) and we decided that this is the true cause of failure in most children. You can go through the "abandonment" syndromes and the "separation anxieties" and blame them for the ADHD (which I personally believe is a crock of crap) and hyperactivity, and in some cases you might be right. These things might be what are making some children fail in school and in life. Then again, you can go back one step and see the real problem. Divorce in America has become so easy.

Irreconcilable differences, such a blameless expression. It means "we tried; we just can't work it out." What it actually means is "we quit, and we aren't even going to put forth much effort."

Back when my parents got married in 1957 there was a toughness in people, a true "no matter what the world throws at us, we are going to get through it, together!" attitude. Where did that go? It went to the lawyers who now have the "I'm going to get you out of this and with half the assets and a nice support check" attitude. I used to mock churchgoing folks for going to classes before marriage to learn how to interact with their spouse, so they could fight and make up, not fight and break up. Oddly, they still have the highest success rate for marriage, nearly double that of people who live without some kind of faith-based moral code.

Then there's crime. No doubt that a single-parent home cuts by half the amount of parental oversight in a child's life. Someone has to work; if you're the only one, I guess it's going to be you.

Unless you go the route of so many and take a handout, Welfare checks. Well, that puts your child at an immediate disadvantage in the early years of his or her life. And it also means you would more than likely live in a lower-income neighborhood that, due to the housing in the area, probably would not have the tax base needed to provide the necessary money to the local school district, thus meaning your kid will go to one of the worse schools in the country, sticking them with yet another strike in the game of life.

Sure, there are exceptions to every rule, and I certainly applaud any single parent, man or woman, who has struggled against these standards and overcome to produce a good child who is willing and able to become a productive part of society. But it is the average outcome of these circumstances that must be looked at with clear eyes. Divorce has put a great many people in these situations. Now, more than ever, fifty years or so after it became near epidemic, divorce has become the standard, not the exception.

In my day, the early 1980s and 1990s, growing up I knew kids with divorced parents, but never really thought too much about it. One guy was poor, his mom divorced his dad and took all three kids with her, and they suffered from it. Another kid I knew had a stepfather. He seemed fine, and then I found out later his stepdad was molesting him and he nearly took his life over it. That also goes up in odds when you have a stepparent, the abuse factor. Another good friend of mine is currently doing time in prison, his parents were divorced, mom remarried a nice guy, but the kid resented him anyway and went out of his way to get into trouble, probably for attention, who knows for sure.

My point is it's too easy. I know some women are with abusive men and need to get out. Drugs, alcohol, and abuse are legit reasons to call for the check and leave, no doubt about it. But most don't divorce over a real problem, they just give up.

Someone says "I don't know what I want" or "I don't think I want to be married anymore" or "We just don't get along anymore." Well, folks, sorry, but nobody ever said it would be easy. Hell, we all heard from all our friends and family, this is no bed of roses and it takes work.

Most of us who have been married have taken our vows to our partner and God seriously. So what goes wrong? I can't answer that one; it differs from relationship to relationship. It just seems so easy to say "check, please" and walk out the door.

The family has always been the most basic building block of society; remove it and you have modern-day America. But if we can fix this problem, I truly believe that many of the others will subside, maybe not all the way, history teaches us that, but maybe the tide of poverty, crime, and poor education will recede just enough for us to get a handle on the real problems we face as a nation.

Just a thought.

# The United States Constitution

## A Brief Study

The Constitution of the United States of America is a simplistic document by design. I hope to do a study of each section or article in a series. I want to start with the Preamble of the Constitution and move forward. If this has been done before, I apologize but my take on things might differ and the more ideas that are out there, the better.

The Preamble: "We the People of the United States, in Order to form a more perfect Union, establish Justice, insure domestic Tranquility, provide for the common defense, promote the general Welfare, and secure the Blessings of Liberty to ourselves and our Posterity, do ordain and establish this Constitution for the United States of America."

This opening statement is so powerful that to merely skip over it for the "meat" of the document is to disregard the opening ceremonies of every major event in a life. It is to forget the birth of a child, the anniversary of a marriage, or the discovery of the continent in the historical context of an American life. While conception of this document was labored over in the Declaration of Independence and later the Articles of Confederation, its birth and that of the nation started with these fifty-two words. How fitting that every state, the capitol city of Washington DC, and the country as a whole is represented in this founding document's numerical value.

It begins with a statement of whom: "We the People." Nowhere in the history of the world has such a founding document owed to its people its very existence. In every other country on earth any documentation recounting its origins has been given to the people, not created by them. The Constitutional Convention delegates were chosen from twelve of the thirteen states to represent their people and their individual state (Rhode Island sent no delegate). It was we who created this country, the very people who would run it, live under its laws, and would preserve it as if it were our own because in fact it was and is our own. "We" would give it life, not have it thrust upon us by others trying to hold us to a preordained station.

Continuing: "of the United States." I want to point out the obvious. Notice the word the is not capitalized. Until the end of the Civil War the states were referred to as "the United States are" instead of the now norm of "the United States is." This stems from the idea that the US was a conglomerate of individual states working in unison for a common purpose, not a centralized national unit divided by geographic bounds. In this we have certainly changed.

Continuing: "in Order to form a more perfect Union." By no means was perfection the ultimate goal as these men understood perfection would not be achieved, but a more perfect union than that as designed under the Articles of Confederation certainly was achievable. The articles lacked the most basic of provisions for allowing the newly formed federalized government to fund its own actions. It was charged with maintaining an army in reserve, but had no way to raise funds to pay for such action. National defense was its most important function and without funds it was destined to fail. It held no real power to legislate with all power reserved for the states. This too was failure in the waiting as the common good could not always be negotiated at the state level.

Continuing: "establish Justice, insure domestic Tranquility, provide for the common defense." These three subjects provide the very reasoning for the preceding statements. There was limited power to create and again, fund a federal judiciary, no provisions by which to insure tranquility, which even today it is a vague reference to "do good and no harm" in essence, and again national defense was underdeveloped. All the more reason to qualify the desire for a "more perfect union." You cannot "provide" that which you are unable to fund.

Continuing: "promote the general Welfare." Now here above all the other provisions in the Preamble do we find the most maligned, misunderstood, and most simplistic to understand statements. The aforementioned "national defense" is preceded by the word provide. This was one of the only responsibilities of the newly formed federal government. However, the word promote is a very different word. When I tell my kids to drive carefully, I am promoting their welfare. When I buy them the car for them to drive, I am providing the car to be driven carefully. When the government funds a research project into cigarette smoking and its possible connection to disease then releases that report to the public, it is promoting the general welfare. When it pays for healthcare, it is providing the general welfare. The differences here are stark and the contrast cannot be ignored. The federal government is to do those things to which it is prescribed and nothing more. Promote versus provide is the proverbial apples and oranges.

Continuing: "and secure the Blessings of Liberty to ourselves and our Posterity." The "Blessings of Liberty" are best defined in my mind as the ability to live without fear of the government bringing upon you undo stress. You should be free to enjoy a life as abundant as you can create without undo stress on the liberty of others. The freedom to create wealth, buy property, build a future for yourself and your children, to make decisions that are best suited to you and your community, and to feel secure in those rights of decision. Your wealth should be able to be passed down to our "Posterity" without fine, without confiscation, and without shame or guilt.

Continuing: "do ordain and establish this Constitution for the United States of America." Ordain is an interesting word, as is establish. To create from the ether a nation that is at the same time the sum total of its parts and standing alone against those who would do it harm. The duality of this nation had never before been conceived. That the power granted the federal government was merely on loan, being sovereign to the states and the people, creates another level of duality. And while republics were not new to the planet, one in which the people themselves sought to create one in order to provide a meaningful institution to work on its behalf was indeed a new concept. Power was shared, or better defined as granted, to the newly formed federal government by the states and people to do their bidding, whereas in the past this power was "granted" temporarily to the people from the ruling classes.

We are a dichotomy of terms. A singular nation of individual states governed by the population that retains as its sovereign right the lending for a time of their personal responsibilities to those duly elected and drawn upon from that same population. While it may seem a mess to the uninitiated, it is truly poetry of trust. ...

But what would I know; I'm just an Average American.

# Article 1—Sections 1, 2, and 3

I am continuing with my series of brief studies of the Constitution by section. Earlier I covered the Preamble, which was no small undertaking. Unfortunately for me, I promised to continue so I have devised a way to do so by breaking down the sections as I see them referencing particular similar content within the document. The makeup of Congress is next. This is contained in Article 1, Sections 1, 2, and 3. Due to the precise nature of each section I will follow each paragraph with my comments.

"Section. 1. All legislative Powers herein granted shall be vested in a Congress of the United States, which shall consist of a Senate and House of Representatives."

It is appropriate that the founders used in particular the word granted in this opening salvo. All power originates with the people in this representative republic. For "powers" to be granted, there must be ownership of those powers to begin with. This "power" is in the ownership of the sovereign kings and queens of any nation and as we Americans are sovereigns of this country, having no king or queen to which we pledge ourselves, it is clear that this power is "granted" by "We the People."

Secondly, the idea of a two-chamber system of legislation owes to the House of Lords and the House of Commons in Great Britain. However, as we do not allow for class identification it was befitting that both the sovereignty of the people and the states be recognized. The Senate is to represent the sovereign interests of the states and to lend a voice in all national matters of importance while the House of Representatives is to provide the same voice in consideration of the sovereignty of the individual people. Today this concept of state sovereignty being of equal import to that of the people is lost on most as they like to claim that senators do not often represent the people's voice in matters. This is because they are not supposed to do so in the first place and it is due to poor civics education and the 17th Amendment (covered later) that most people cannot differentiate between the singular basic duties of either chamber, representation of their prescribed sovereigns.

"Section. 2. The House of Representatives shall be composed of Members chosen every second Year by the People of the several States, and the Electors in each State shall have the Qualifications requisite for Electors of the most numerous Branch of the State Legislature."

Simply put, biennial elections shall take place for House seats. This was done, according to the Federalist Papers (written by Hamilton, Madison, and Jay; Madison, if you will recall, is credited with the largest portion of the Constitution), because:

> It is a received and well-founded maxim, that where no other circumstances affect the case, the greater the power is, the shorter ought to be its duration; and, conversely, the smaller the power, the more safely may its duration be protracted. In the second place, it has, on another occasion, been shown that the federal legislature will not only be restrained by its dependence on its people, as other legislative bodies are, but that it will be, moreover, watched and controlled by the several collateral legislatures, which other legislative bodies are not. And in the third place, no comparison can be made between the means that will be possessed by the more permanent branches of the federal government for seducing, if they should be disposed to seduce, the House of Representatives from their duty to the people, and the means of influence over the popular branch possessed by the other branches of the government above cited. With less power, therefore, to abuse, the federal representatives can be less tempted on one side, and will be doubly watched on the other.

It could have been three years or twelve, but with the power granted being so close to the level of the people themselves, it was admitted that the more often the election, the faster the changes in national thought would be represented in the chamber from which all legislation is to be fostered. This is the reason why we should not need term limits. We the people are the mechanism for term limits if only we prescribe to the original intent of the Constitution.

You will also notice that those elected must have "the Qualifications requisite for Electors of the most numerous Branch of the State Legislature." This ensures that those capable of sitting in office in the House are of the same merit as those representing the people in the day-to-day decision making in the state houses. However, as we will see, this alone was not the sole requirement to serve.

"No Person shall be a Representative who shall not have attained to the Age of twenty-five Years, and been seven Years a Citizen of the United States, and who shall not, when elected, be an Inhabitant of that State in which he shall be chosen."

Twenty-five years of age may today seem young to represent the people, but I disagree. They are of every right and responsibility as the seventy-five-year-old under the definitions of adult and citizen in this country. More so many argue to this day that no "chosen" citizen should be permitted to serve, as was once debated at the convention. But those who chose to be citizens instead of being born to that status by luck or the grace of God are granted every equality to those born into citizenship (save for serving as the chief executive), as it should be. Often as we have found in these later centuries, their memories of tyranny are not so far removed as ours as they oftentimes have escaped it within their own lifetime and are quicker to recognize it than we of birthright.

> Representatives and direct Taxes shall be apportioned among the several States which may be included within this Union, according to their respective Numbers, which shall be determined by adding to the whole Number of free Persons, including those bound to Service for a Term of Years, and excluding Indians not taxed, three fifths of all other Persons (Modified by 14th Amendment). The actual Enumeration shall be made within three Years after the first Meeting of the Congress of the United States, and within every subsequent Term of ten Years, in such Manner as they shall by Law direct. The Number of Representatives shall not exceed one for every thirty Thousand, but each State shall have at Least one Representative; and until such enumeration shall be made, the State of New Hampshire shall be entitled to chuse three, Massachusetts eight, Rhode-Island and

Providence Plantations one, Connecticut five, New-York six, New Jersey four, Pennsylvania eight, Delaware one, Maryland six, Virginia ten, North Carolina five, South Carolina five, and Georgia three.

Here we have the duty of the census. That every ten years shall a count be taken to ensure representation is adequate and that those lines of demarcation are appropriate in representation. Until fixing the number of representatives in 1911, seats were added each census that showed increases in population and in accordance with the fair representation of each district to as near an equal population as could be done. Had this not been fixed at 435 members we would today, based on a population of some three hundred million, have a House of some ten thousand members. Might that have been better or worse I will leave in your hands to decide. In following the Constitution that each state has at least one representative the 435 number was increased to allow for Alaska and Hawaii to be represented until the districts were reapportioned following the 1960 Census.

At this time the 3/5 clause must be mentioned, despite it no longer having authority in the Constitution with the passage of the 14th Amendment. It must be noted that America was not perfect from the start, and the prejudices of the day were incorporated at its start. But it cannot go without mention that the 14th Amendment shows that the Founding Fathers were aware that those things that were inconsistent with "Liberty for All" would be addressed by later Americans, bringing the document in question closer to that dream of perfection. The 14th Amendment makes consistent those goals as enumerated in the Preamble.

"When vacancies happen in the Representation from any State, the Executive Authority thereof shall issue Writs of Election to fill such Vacancies."

Again we see that the sovereign right of the state is recognized in the Constitution with the sole power to fill vacancies the responsibility of the state to fill. This is no small matter and should not be overlooked. The federal government cannot pick and chose the representation of the people or the states. This also brings into sharp focus the idea of from whom the power is granted and to whom the federal government is beholden.

"The House of Representatives shall chuse [sic] their Speaker and other Officers; and shall have the sole Power of Impeachment."

This refers simply but eloquently to the power to self-regulate the administration of the chamber itself. It is brought into sharper focus in Section 4. The House will set the rules by which it engages in action with no undue influence from either the Senate, the states, the executive or judiciary branches, nor from the people themselves. As this power to assemble has been granted by the people and the states it was best agreed that those in the chamber be allowed to organize their procedures within the limits of the Constitution itself. Impeachment is to begin here in the House as the House will act as the prosecutors in any impeachment trial. The trial itself is to be held in the Senate and will be covered in Section 3.

"Section. 3. The Senate of the United States shall be composed of two Senators from each State, chosen by the Legislature thereof (Modified by 17th Amendment), for six Years; and each Senator shall have one Vote."

Prior to the 17th Amendment the states' legislatures chose who would represent the states in the federal system. I believe it was a poor decision to change this law, although having been done by amendment it certainly contains within it no illegality. My thought process is simple: Because the people now directly attend to the election of the state representative, the states are no longer represented as sovereigns but are represented by proxy. There is a general disagreement on this and I land firmly on one side of it. It is thought by the other side that the direct election of the state representative makes them more beholden to the people of those states and that they are more likely to therefore respond to the needs of the people. It is that very argument that fuels my opposition to it because the Senate's purpose was to provide adequate representation of the states as equal to that of the people.

Immediately after they shall be assembled in Consequence of the first Election, they shall be divided as equally as may be into three Classes. The Seats of the Senators of the first Class shall be vacated at the Expiration of the second Year, of the second Class at the Expiration of the fourth Year, and of the third Class at the Expiration of the sixth Year, so that one third may be chosen every second Year; and if Vacancies happen by Resignation, or otherwise, during the Recess of the Legislature of any State, the Executive thereof may make temporary Appointments until the next Meeting of the Legislature, which shall then fill such Vacancies (Modified by 17th Amendment).

This section provides for a staggered end date of all terms. In England, at the time our Constitution was penned, Parliament was dissolved at the end of each five-year term and forced to start over with new elections and/or appointments. In order to resist a restart of sorts at the end of each term, a staggered approach was introduced to ensure continuity to the people's business.

Passed under pressure from the people themselves (which does not force me to agree with the decision), the 17th Amendment was passed after thirty-one of the thirty-two states required had requested a Constitutional Convention. Had its passage not quelled those requests, all portions of the Constitution would have been open for revision, which would have transformed the document in perhaps more harmful a manner than conceding to the people themselves. But in the end it still stripped from the states real representation in my opinion due to the unequaled pressure of the citizen versus the obligation to defend the state in the federal system, even from the people. Remember, personal and state sovereignty were to be equally represented.

"No Person shall be a Senator who shall not have attained to the Age of thirty Years, and been nine Years a Citizen of the United States, and who shall not, when elected, be an Inhabitant of that State for which he shall be chosen."

Similar to the House requirements is was thought that since the term of service was extended beyond that of the House members, and since these senators were being chosen by legislators as opposed to the common man, their ability to serve would be greater than those in the House as their election was by like-mannered public servants. (Another issue I have with the 17th Amendment is that it did not also revise their terms in accordance with the changes under which they are now elected.) In other words, it was thought that most senators would be chosen from the very members of the legislatures choosing them and would be better qualified for a longer term. The age of thirty-five was for the most part simply to ensure greater experience for the longer term of service.

"The Vice President of the United States shall be President of the Senate, but shall have no Vote, unless they be equally divided."

Some claim this has given undue influence to the executive to meddle in the practices of the Senate but in reality it was to deaden deadlocks so that the people's business could not be stalemated by the disagreement of a split chamber.

"The Senate shall chuse [sic] their other Officers, and also a President pro tempore, in the Absence of the Vice President, or when he shall exercise the Office of President of the United States."

Again as before, because the states vested their representation (which we established they no longer have as they once did) the chamber would be best suited to devise and maintain their own operational guidelines within the constraints of the Constitution. Interestingly, a few vice presidents have spent as much time serving as presidents and overseeing the activities unless otherwise engaged. Truman once complained he did not want to just "go to weddings and funerals."

"The Senate shall have the sole Power to try all Impeachments. When sitting for that Purpose, they shall be on Oath or Affirmation. When the President of the United States is tried, the Chief Justice shall preside: And no Person shall be convicted without the Concurrence of two thirds of the Members present."

Bringing in the chief justice of the Supreme Court was really a novel idea here. It provided that both the opposing branches would be present and offer authority to the proceedings should the executive need to be removed from office. The House must begin this process with a majority vote to bring impeachment charges and play the part of prosecutor in the Senate. The Senate must conclude by a two-thirds vote that the president is guilty (although not legally) for his removal. The vice president as president of the Senate runs the impeachment of all other elected parties subject to impeachment except the president because his impartiality cannot be assured, having served with and being in line for the presidency himself depending on the results.

"Judgment in Cases of Impeachment shall not extend further than to removal from Office, and disqualification to hold and enjoy any Office of honor, Trust or Profit under the United States: but the Party convicted shall nevertheless be liable and subject to Indictment, Trial, Judgment and Punishment, according to Law."

This is simply a statement that impeachment is not a conclusion of guilt or innocence of a crime as the Senate cannot pass judgment as a legal court. It can only provide that those impeached are to be removed and that this removal is not a legal mechanism providing for guilt or innocence in the eyes of the law. And as such, it does not cause the individual to be safe from actual legal ramifications; they are not above the law. President Clinton learned this when it was determined he lied about his affair with Monica Lewinsky under oath. As a result, the State Bar of Arkansas stripped him of his license to practice law because it is against the law to lie under oath.

# Sections 4, 5, 6, and 7

Continuing with the Constitution, we move into Sections 4, 5, 6, and 7 of Article 1. But before we do there is an urgent matter that must be addressed. It is one of meaning. There are two words in particular that must be observed in their proper context and these words are shall and not. Shall means only one thing: will. It does not mean might, should, could, ought, would, maybe, or kind of. It means "will," as in it will be done. There is no interpretation to the word at all. Not means only one thing as well: no. When placed together, creating the term shall not, it means will no(t). It does not mean should not unless, could not unless, would not unless, might not unless, and ought not unless. ... It simply means what it says: Shall Not!

"Section. 4. The Times, Places and Manner of holding Elections for Senators and Representatives, shall be prescribed in each State by the Legislature thereof; but the Congress may at any time by Law make or alter such Regulations, except as to the Places of chusing Senators."

Does this remind you of the argument I made earlier about the 17th Amendment? This is one of those sections remanded to history by the passage of that Amendment. Although not suggested in most texts it clearly was affected. "Times, Places and Manner of holding Elections of Senators," these were repealed under the 17th Amendment as prior to that they were prescribed by all states to be chosen in the state legislature's largest chamber. It continues, "shall be prescribed in each State by the Legislature thereof." "Shall"—what a powerful little word! However, I will concede that it clearly says that Congress has the power to change this "except as to the Places of chusing Senators." That place was in those state chambers. Now it is done directly by the people in popular elections, thus stripping the sovereignty of the states away. It is my suggestion that the 17th Amendment is by rights unconstitutional and should be reversed.

"The Congress shall assemble at least once in every Year, and such Meeting shall be on the first Monday in December, unless they shall by Law appoint a different Day."

Simple in it clarity, Congress "shall" meet yearly. This is in reference to Parliament again, which was known not to meet for years at a stretch because some sovereigns (kings) saw no need to include the people in the decision-making process. In fact, that was the king's right under their established laws. It was therefore decided that considering the fact that we are the sovereigns of this country and our power is vested above all others within the legislature that necessity dictated that the people's voice (the king's voice) was to be heard, at the very least, yearly. Notice no provision was mentioned of "unless otherwise changed" or "unless the executive decides differently." It was the vested powers of the people that "shall" be heard.

"Section. 5. Each House shall be the Judge of the Elections, Returns and Qualifications of its own Members, and a Majority of each shall constitute a Quorum to do Business; but a smaller Number may adjourn from day to day, and may be authorized to compel the Attendance of absent Members, in such Manner, and under such Penalties as each House may provide."

Do you remember a few years back when several members of Congress walked out and there were rumors that they might be arrested and forced back into the chamber? This is where that idea comes from. The Congressional Chambers, both the House and Senate, set their own rules. Again, in reference to our powers being vested in them and their need to create procedures to operate. A quorum is the minimum number that must be present for any legislation to be passed. It states clearly, "a majority of each constitutes a Quorum." This was done to ensure minority rule was not implemented. Imagine if only three (enough to stop a deadlock) were needed to pass legislation.

"Each House may determine the Rules of its Proceedings, punish its Members for disorderly Behaviour, and, with the Concurrence of two thirds, expel a Member."

This seems open to a lot of interpretation. Congress creates the rules of its proceedings, prescribes punishment, and can kick a member out? That last part sounds inviting but has it ever been done? It has. Twenty times, seventeen during the Civil War for siding with the Confederacy. In 2002 Jim Traficant was expelled after his conviction of bribery and tax evasion, and in 1980 Michael Myers was removed for bribery as well. Only once has treason been the reason and that was way back in 1797. Perhaps this is something we need to pay closer attention to these days.

All in all, it is necessary for Congress to have these abilities to self-police and to get the work of the people done without fear of bribes and collusion. (Sorry, had to laugh at that a bit, too bad we no longer take that part seriously ... no really, it's too bad for us.)

Each House shall keep a Journal of its Proceedings, and from time to time publish the same, excepting such Parts as may in their Judgment require Secrecy; and the Yeas and Nays of the Members of either House on any question shall, at the Desire of one fifth of those Present, be entered on the Journal."

Let's be honest, transparency has never been a real strong suit with Congress. But that is a good thing. Remember, whatever we know, our enemies know, especially today with 24/7 cable news and the New York Times eager to tell the world when we do anything not completely within their definition of ethical. Congress must keep a journal of its proceedings and today they do for every vote, except those dealing with national security (even those are maintained somewhere, just not open to the public for viewing). I don't believe that desire of one-fifth of either house is really needed these days to keep track. They still have the occasional voice vote, but it is usually not on the actual bill itself for final passage, just on procedural aspects of their business.

"Neither House, during the Session of Congress, shall, without the Consent of the other, adjourn for more than three days, nor to any other Place than that in which the two Houses shall be sitting."

Put plainly, both houses of Congress must agree on vacation time. That's all this means.

"Section. 6. The Senators and Representatives shall receive a Compensation for their Services, to be ascertained by Law, and paid out of the Treasury of the United States. They shall in all Cases, except Treason, Felony and Breach of the Peace, be privileged from Arrest during their Attendance at the Session of their respective Houses, and in going to and returning from the same; and for any Speech or Debate in either House, they shall not be questioned in any other Place."

Anyone doing a job should be paid. And anyone doing a job for the American people should be compensated for their time away from home. They are paid by the people out of the people's money through the treasury. The law states clearly that they are immune from prosecution only while serving, unless for reasons of treason, felony, bribery, or breach of peace. Breach of peace may have to be better defined. Law dictionaries define it as: "breach of peace: essentially, this refers to public misbehavior, such as becoming drunk and disorderly, playing loud music in a residential area between the hours of 11 PM and 7 AM, or instigating a civil disturbance such as a riot. This is better known as disturbing the peace, or public disorder, and is a misdemeanor in most jurisdictions." While I am fairly sure the founders were not talking about stereos being played too loud, the rest makes perfect sense. Does this mean they are above the law? No, it does not. It means they are clear during the people's business only; in going or coming from the Hill or when actually there. Nothing more and certainly nothing less.

"No Senator or Representative shall, during the Time for which he was elected, be appointed to any civil Office under the Authority of the United States, which shall have been created, or the Emoluments whereof shall have been encreased during such time: and no Person holding any Office under the United States, shall be a Member of either House during his Continuance in Office."

This is the reason you never have a senator run for president, win, and then vote in the Senate Hall. You cannot hold two offices at any one time. If there was a change to this I wish it would be this: "No member shall, while in the service of elected office, attempt election to another office without having first relinquished the appointment of the first." Had the Founding Fathers thought that public service would be as padded with benefits as it is now, I feel certain that this would have been added. (Right after they raised much hell about the idea of the benefits outside of direct compensation.)

"Section. 7. All Bills for raising Revenue shall originate in the House of Representatives; but the Senate may propose or concur with Amendments as on other Bills."

Simply put, the House begins all tax increases, although the Senate may start the process and work in conjunction with the

House. If only they had placed a passing percentage of 66 percent of the vote for revenue bills ... However, that would have been stupid considering the government needs to be able to raise revenue to cover needed expenditures. Our problem today isn't that the government spends too much it is that the government does too much and therefore spends much more than they would if they were constricted as the Constitution prescribed them to be.

> Every Bill which shall have passed the House of Representatives and the Senate, shall, before it become a Law, be presented to the President of the United States; if he approve he shall sign it, but if not he shall return it, with his Objections to that House in which it shall have originated, who shall enter the Objections at large on their Journal, and proceed to reconsider it. If after such Reconsideration two thirds of that House shall agree to pass the Bill, it shall be sent, together with the Objections, to the other House, by which it shall likewise be reconsidered, and if approved by two thirds of that House, it shall become a Law. But in all such Cases the Votes of both Houses shall be determined by Yeas and Nays, and the Names of the Persons voting for and against the Bill shall be entered on the Journal of each House respectively. If any Bill shall not be returned by the President within ten Days (Sundays excepted) after it shall have been presented to him, the Same shall be a Law, in like Manner as if he had signed it, unless the Congress by their Adjournment prevent its Return, in which Case it shall not be a Law.

American Government 101. Congress passes a bill in both houses; it proceeds to the president for his signature. If he signs it, the bill is law; if he vetoes it, it returns for further debate and alteration to either be in line with the president's wishes or it can be voted on by Congress again. If both chambers pass it by two-thirds of the vote the veto is overridden and it becomes law without the president's approval. If the president does not want to make waves he can let it sit on his desk for two weeks and it becomes law anyway, as if he signed it. The only exception is if Congress adjourns prior to the ten-day time period and is unable to receive the bill in question.

The interesting thing to me is that the president is given two weeks to read it before signing it. Yet Congress is often required to vote on bills they have never read and could not read in ten days if they tried. Something to think about ...

> Every Order, Resolution, or Vote to which the Concurrence of the Senate and House of Representatives may be necessary (except on a question of Adjournment) shall be presented to the President of the United States; and before the Same shall take Effect, shall be approved by him, or being disapproved by him, shall be re-passed by two thirds of the Senate and House of Representatives, according to the Rules and Limitations prescribed in the Case of a Bill.

Again, further explanation of American Government 101.

Most of what you just read was in response to problems within Parliament in Great Britain over the one hundred years prior to the drafting of the US Constitution. Still more waits. But as Parliament sometimes went decades without being called to order and the people's voice was granted by the king, not protected by him, some very real constraint was necessarily placed on the federal government to ensure there was no misunderstanding from where its temporary power would come. I call it temporary because only temporary assignment of limited power can be granted any man who chooses to serve his fellow man in his absence. That is the power vested in the individual who is there for the moment.

Lasting or perpetual power was granted by the people to the document itself as the law of the land, created by the people with their consent. The creator always retains the ultimate right and responsibility to change, extract from, or add to any creation their toil creates. This is what keeps Americans as a whole in the position of ultimate power if only we would exercise it. We are the creator of this document, of this government, and of these independent yet United States.

The monarchs of Europe well understood what was being claimed by these people. They knew full well that Americans were claiming for themselves the very birthright of the "great kings and queens" of out collective mother countries. They also knew it would empower America in ways not even considered as their power would have to be reduced in order to lift the people to equal status. We had no kings, we had no "ruling class" (except between races, which we later corrected), and we offered no allegiance to anyone but ourselves, our flag, and to each other. True freedom, it was discovered, came from a mind-set of equality, not a piece of paper, but that paper did allow us to continue the freedom we claimed and pass it to our children. Imagine you have been a subject for your entire life, then you wake up one day and you are free. You can go where you want, do what you want, own land, vote, and be a part of the process deciding your future.

Too many people never really consider the ground-shattering change this idea was after one thousand years of monarchical oppression. Yet in a generation we were on our way.

## Section 8

It is here in Article 1, Section 8, that we begin to understand the limitations and specific areas of responsibility that Congress will have in this new union.

"Section. 8. The Congress shall have Power To lay and collect Taxes, Duties, Imposts and Excises, to pay the Debts and provide for the common Defence and general Welfare of the United States; but all Duties, Imposts and Excises shall be uniform throughout the United States."

As a matter of necessity and following the debacle that was the Articles of Confederation it was understood by most men in attendance that in order to run a government it must have the ability to acquire revenue. In the infinite wisdom of the founders was this little gem, "but all Duties, Imposts and Excises shall be uniform throughout the United States." It was in this statement alone that it was clearly indicated that no state would have either favorable of unfavorable status among the states.

Also in this statement we see for the first and only time the following: "to pay the Debts and provide for the common Defence and general Welfare of the United States." Clearly, in this statement we see a difference in wording when referring to the "general Welfare," however, this is not to suggest that "providing" welfare was the intent. Promoting the general welfare, as we saw in the Preamble, was the intent as it was relayed in the opening statement. A good liberal would cling to this section if they were worth their salt, but they never seem to do so, mostly because few have read beyond the Preamble. Still, it is bothersome that provide precedes general welfare; however, with the lack of import placed on the words general and common both words should be taken in their purest form. For instance, "common" suggests "pertaining or belonging equally to an entire community, nation, or culture" while "general" would suggest "of, pertaining to, or true of such persons or things in the main, with possible exceptions; common to most; prevalent; usual." Notice "common to most"; it indicates that general does not include all aspects of a person's life, just those things in common to most. In this case I would suggest that includes life, liberty, and the pursuit of happiness, not a general common check made out to you by Uncle Sam at the expense of your countrymen.

"To borrow Money on the credit of the United States."

Someone had to be able to borrow in cases of emergency, war, or economic need. Unfortunately, this power has been badly abused and all the Congress really does anymore in this regard is raise the debt ceiling as they have done to over $13 trillion. This also, in my opinion, clearly indicates that the Federal Reserve, a private banking organization, has no business issuing our money or running our banking system. This is Congress's job, clearly.

"To regulate Commerce with foreign Nations, and among the several States, and with the Indian Tribes."

Here it is, the Hail Mary of all congressional oversight. It is from this clause that Congress meddles into just about every aspect of our lives. If a gun is sold over state lines, BAM!, you have to register it (although today several states are passing legislation right down the center of this clause claiming that if a firearm is manufactured and sold within the same state it would not fall under this section of Article 1—a brilliant move). Insurance companies can't sell interstate policies because of legislation based on this clause and it was this clause that Congress cited when passing Prohibition. Likewise it is this clause that I cite when suggesting Congress back out of the law stopping interstate insurance sales just as they did the 18th Amendment.

"To establish an uniform Rule of Naturalization, and uniform Laws on the subject of Bankruptcies throughout the United States."

Immigration legislation, you will notice, is not mentioned here, only "Rules of Naturalization." Chew on that for few minutes. Immigration, if we are to believe the Constitution, specifically the Bill of Rights, would be considered a state right because "The powers not delegated to the United States by the Constitution, nor prohibited by it to the States, are reserved to the States respectively, or to the people" (10th Amendment found in the Bill of Rights).

As for bankruptcy we can all be glad that the laws are uniform, I guess, as many of us are now becoming acquainted with them....

"To coin Money, regulate the Value thereof, and of foreign Coin, and fix the Standard of Weights and Measures."

These, of course, are the powers granted to Congress, not the Federal Reserve. The monster of Jekyl Island continues to cause us as much grief today as it did at its inception. Google Jekyl Island and Federal Reserve and enjoy a fantasy story that became a horror story.

"To provide for the Punishment of counterfeiting the Securities and current Coin of the United States."

It does not say "ordain counterfeiting" yet many believe that is exactly what happened with the Federal Reserve Act of 1913. By the way, this little ditty also gave us the income tax....

"To establish Post Offices and post Roads."

Ah, yes, the only nonmilitary entity Congress was mandated to create. And has it not turned out wonderfully? We needed a way to transport mail around the nation and it was a sound idea, before the unions, politicians, and other Irish Welfare recipients got involved. (Irish Welfare is a dated term meaning government employee.)

"To promote the Progress of Science and useful Arts, by securing for limited Times to Authors and Inventors the exclusive Right to their respective Writings and Discoveries."

Here we again run into the word promote and, even better, a definition of what they meant by it: "by securing for limited Times to Authors and Inventors the exclusive Right to their respective Writings and Discoveries." Now if we again look back to "Promote the General Welfare" as found in the Preamble, it appears to be along the same lines as promote used in this section. By allowing authors and other artists the exclusive rights for a limited time to their works they were allowed exclusive profit from its use. It also allows inventors the same ability to profit from their discoveries. This means actually promoting personal ownership of what one creates. If applied to welfare, would it not indicate that those who promote a general welfare are really there to ensure that you have exclusivity to what you own, create, use, etc.?

"To constitute Tribunals inferior to the supreme Court."

This they actually did with great success. It is the manner in which they are now populated that we may have an issue with.

"To define and punish Piracies and Felonies committed on the high Seas, and Offences against the Law of Nations."

In order to have "teeth" Congress had to have an ability to back up the law with consequences of breaking them.

"To declare War, grant Letters of Marque and Reprisal, and make Rules concerning Captures on Land and Water."

This ensured that the people were represented in all matters before, during, and following any war. The president can execute the war effort but the people to whom he reports must be actively involved in the spoils of that war.

"To raise and support Armies, but no Appropriation of Money to that Use shall be for a longer Term than two Years."

Again, this is in direct relation to the fall of the Articles of Confederation. In that document, too, Congress was instructed to provide for war, but was given no way to do so. The two-year limit from what I have read was really a safeguard against a rouge presidency dragging out for this reason, a war of aggression.

"To provide and maintain a Navy."

Six words, pretty straightforward, but again so too was the Articles of Confederation on the subject just minus the ability to actually do so.

"To make Rules for the Government and Regulation of the land and naval Forces."

Don't get hung up on the wording directly, this applies to all manner of military from army to air force. Keep in mind Orville and Wilbur had not yet made flight a prospect of war.

"To provide for calling forth the Militia to execute the Laws of the Union, suppress Insurrections and repel Invasions."

This one needs some time spent on it. "Militia"—what exactly does that mean? Liberals like to accuse those in favor of 2nd Amendment rights extending to personal ownership of guns of misunderstanding what a "well-regulated militia" is. In the 2nd Amendment it spells out clearly that "A well regulated Militia, being necessary to the security of a free State, the right of the people to keep and bear Arms, shall not be infringed." You do not see the words "as part of" referring to the ownership of the individual corresponding to the militia as being necessary.

The idea that a state militia would consist of any particular quarter of society is not defined within the Constitution and for good reason. Refer back to the 10th Amendment: "The powers not delegated to the United States by the Constitution, nor prohibited by it to the States, are reserved to the States respectively, or to the people." Clearly any state regulation was to be at the state's fancy. However, Congress was given the right to call upon these people of whatever state definition to fight in case of invasion or insurrection. It has been tested many times but with no clear cut answers ... perhaps "insurrection" has yet to be quantified.

"To provide for organizing, arming, and disciplining, the Militia, and for governing such Part of them as may be employed in the Service of the United States, reserving to the States respectively, the Appointment of the Officers, and the Authority of training the Militia according to the discipline prescribed by Congress."

This spells out so clearly the point at which congressional oversight of the militia is to be forthcoming. "[A]s may be employed in the Service of the United States" tells me that not until such time as they are called upon to serve in the name of the United States is the federal government permitted to place any rules or regulations upon them, yet even after this situation arises, the states retain the right to name the officers and retain the training as it is needed or prescribed by Congress. Who is clearly suborned to whom?

> To exercise exclusive Legislation in all Cases whatsoever, over such District (not exceeding ten Miles square) as may, by Cession of particular States, and the Acceptance of Congress, become the Seat of the Government of the United States, and to exercise like Authority over all Places purchased by the Consent of the Legislature of the State in which the Same shall be, for the Erection of Forts, Magazines, Arsenals, dock-Yards, and other needful Buildings.

The capital city, as is necessary, is under the direct control of Congress. This created Washington DC for all intents and purposes. And with that creation came the sole responsibility of running the Capitol. I ask you, if Washington DC is under direct congressional control would it not be fair to say that every piece of legislation regarding its management is a window into the ability of Congress to lead and manage?

"To make all Laws which shall be necessary and proper for carrying into Execution the foregoing Powers, and all other Powers vested by this Constitution in the Government of the United States, or in any Department or Officer thereof."

This is the clause used to justify the Federal Reserve and all other departments within the federal government. Congress can create at will any department it wants or believes necessary, but all others outside of the Federal Reserve have one thing in common, they are under the direct and common oversight of Congress. The Federal Reserve is not. It is for this reason and this reason alone that the argument can be made that the Federal Reserve is in direct violation of constitutional law.

This is also where the FBI, CIA, post office, ATF, and a host of others are granted their power to enforce the laws of the land. It needs to be done this way as all are acting on behalf of the very people who created the document on which the system was build. However, it does not need to be as wide of scope as it is today.

# Sections 9 and 10

"Section. 9. The Migration or Importation of such Persons as any of the States now existing shall think proper to admit, shall not be prohibited by the Congress prior to the Year one thousand eight hundred and eight, but a Tax or duty may be imposed on such Importation, not exceeding ten dollars for each Person."

This statement dealt with the taxation assessed on slaves as they were imported into the various slave states in the South. What many people do not recognize is that one of the many reasons leading to the Civil War is found here. According to this clause, no tariffs were to exist beyond 1808, yet compromise after compromise extended those tariffs (taxes) on the slave states. The facts are that slavery was winding down anyway as the numbers of slave owners in those states bordering the South were slowly but surely moving away from slavery. Cotton was king in the South and the number of workers needed to produce the White

Oil was not as necessary with the invention of the cotton gin by Eli Whitney. Even Lincoln saw this and said as much in the 1858 "House Divided Speech" when he said, "arrest the further spread of it, and place it where the public mind shall rest in the belief that it is in the course of ultimate extinction." He expected as most did that it was a dying situation anyway. But before Lincoln was even placed in office seven states had left the Union.

A newly elected president of the Union had little choice but to preserve the Union itself. The Dred Scott decision, which said that Scott had no standing in the Supreme Court because he was in fact a slave and slaves had no rights, should have quelled the South as it also said the federal government had no power to compel the states to stay in the Union. I am sure you can see where the president and the Supreme Court were at odds with each other. The die was really cast when the Kansas Nebraska Act was passed in 1854 stating that states could vote for or against slavery. Lincoln, tariffs, and Dred Scott were just kindling on an already hot bed of embers.

Many in the North wanted the practice stopped, and so did many Southerners. But the issue was pushed when Lincoln won the election because the South was already feeling weakened in Congress as less representation was now available supporting their desire to continue with slavery. With Lincoln they thought for sure that Congress would override their desires and that secession was the only means to maintain their livelihoods.

"The Privilege of the Writ of Habeas Corpus shall not be suspended, unless when in Cases of Rebellion or Invasion the public Safety may require it."

"Writ of Habeas Corpus" says that you cannot be held without cause. You have the right to ask why and you have a right to your day in court.

Although it has been suspended under many other circumstances, from the Civil War to Roosevelt's Second World War when Asians (specifically Japanese) were interred in camps throughout the West, there should be no real reason for any citizen to fear this statement. It protects us from a runaway government that believes it grants us the rights instead of us granting it the power. In these cases "the public Safety may require it" was the roundabout. Lincoln was tiring (as we are today) of media telegraphing the next punch during the Civil War and Roosevelt was sure the Japanese walking around were out to get us. Forget about the Germans in this country, it was just the Japanese Roosevelt worried about. Roosevelt's mistake, like Lincoln's, was that they applied the suspension to law-abiding citizens and not just foreign nationals who by all rights are not covered by the Constitution. Bush, on the other hand, applied it correctly by never considering it in the first place and never bringing terrorist suspects onto US soil, except in Cuba where they have been held pending military tribunal.

"No Bill of Attainder or ex post facto Law shall be passed."

A Bill of Attainder would be a law passed stating that all (Black, Whites, Jews, one-legged monkey-looking men) of one group are by definition guilty of a crime. Ex post facto means no retroactive law can be passed. This would be like saying riding a bike on Tuesday is against the law now and it applies to Roger who we saw last week (a week before the law was passed) riding on Tuesday so he has to go to jail.

"No Capitation, or other direct, Tax shall be laid, unless in Proportion to the Census or Enumeration herein before directed to be taken."

This says that no tax (capitation) can be levied on a person nor can indirect taxes (taxes levied on an event, think income) be passed. At least this is how it was read at the time. But all that ended with the 16th Amendment: "The Congress shall have power to lay and collect taxes on incomes, from whatever source derived, without apportionment among the several States, and without regard to any census or enumeration," which clarified what could be taxes, how it was to be defined, and who would have to pay it. Ratification took time but it was ratified despite many who claim it was not.

"No Tax or Duty shall be laid on Articles exported from any State."

This holds true today, between the states. You are not taxed on items you ship to Georgia, nor are those items taxed when coming from Georgia (using Georgia as any state). Items shipped out of the country are also not taxed from what I can find. (If I am wrong on this account, please let me know. I can find no information on it.)

"No Preference shall be given by any Regulation of Commerce or Revenue to the Ports of one State over those of another: nor shall Vessels bound to, or from, one State, be obliged to enter, clear or pay Duties in another."

This says the federal government cannot have a preferred port that charges lower taxes (duties, tariffs) than any other port in the country. It also says that if you ship something from one state to another no tax can be charged. However, duty can be charged on items imported from out of the country when they arrive on our shores. But it must be equal in all states.

"No Money shall be drawn from the Treasury, but in Consequence of Appropriations made by Law; and a regular Statement and Account of Receipts and Expenditures of all public Money shall be published from time to time."

Only Congress can take money from the treasury to run the country's affairs, no one else can access federal dollars. Not the president and not the Supreme Court and not the states. However, their idea of publishing an account from time to time is a joke today. This should have included a clause stating that "unless in a time of war, no money can be expended beyond that which is in the treasury." But, alas, it did not make it in there, and now let me introduce you to our $13 trillion national debt.

"No Title of Nobility shall be granted by the United States: And no Person holding any Office of Profit or Trust under them, shall, without the Consent of the Congress, accept of any present, Emolument, Office, or Title, of any kind whatever, from any King, Prince, or foreign State."

We don't do knighthood, or any other title outside of "citizen" in this country. We are all equal. We are not allowed to accept it from any other country either.

"Section. 10. No State shall enter into any Treaty, Alliance, or Confederation; grant Letters of Marque and Reprisal; coin Money; emit Bills of Credit; make any Thing but gold and silver Coin a Tender in Payment of Debts; pass any Bill of Attainder, ex post facto Law, or Law impairing the Obligation of Contracts, or grant any Title of Nobility."

The claim that the states cannot do these particular things makes sense. Only one common voice should speak on behalf of the nation as a whole when dealing with money, alliances, and contracts covering the nation. The gold or silver coin part was before the change to worthless paper money. Now there's some change we could believe in....

It also makes clear that by joining the Union no state could pass retroactive laws or make groups subject to special law. This could well be the cornerstone for overturning all the equal opportunity and hate crime legislation if it were done correctly.

"No State shall, without the Consent of the Congress, lay any Imposts or Duties on Imports or Exports, except what may be absolutely necessary for executing it's inspection Laws: and the net Produce of all Duties and Imposts, laid by any State on Imports or Exports, shall be for the Use of the Treasury of the United States; and all such Laws shall be subject to the Revision and Controul (Old English Spelling) of the Congress."

Only Congress can set import duties (taxes) on incoming freight. However, states can charge for costs associated with carrying out federally mandated inspections. However, if they take in more than the cost of the inspection, Uncle Sam gets the difference.

"No State shall, without the Consent of Congress, lay any Duty of Tonnage, keep Troops, or Ships of War in time of Peace, enter into any Agreement or Compact with another State, or with a foreign Power, or engage in War, unless actually invaded, or in such imminent Danger as will not admit of delay."

The states handed over military defense to the national government, one of the only things they actually agreed to hand over. That is constitutional. No state can wage war against another state. The only time a state is allowed to do anything militarily is if they cannot reach Congress in time for a national response and must, in the interest of time, defend themselves. This is no longer an issue with modern communications.

This concludes Article 1 of the US Constitution. So we now understand what Congress is supposed to do and, more importantly, what they are not supposed to do. I would be interested if anyone can find me the following provisions in Article 1: congressional power over education, energy, immigration, healthcare, automotive fuel emissions, gun registration and sales, employment standards, or environmental regulation.

Please use these in your references....

# Article 2—Sections 1, 2, 3, and 4

"Section. 1. The executive Power shall be vested in a President of the United States of America. He shall hold his Office during the Term of four Years, and, together with the Vice President, chosen for the same Term, be elected, as follows."

Notice first the words "executive Powers shall be vested." This is to say that these powers of the people and the states are to be vested or placed temporarily in one person for a specific period of time. That period of time is to be determined not by term limits but by a vote of the people. Four years accounts for an adequate amount of time for on-the-job training and a full understanding of the position along with some governance. Term limits are completely at odds with the idea of a free society that chooses their leaders from amongst themselves.

It suggests that the vice president is elected in the same manner as the first. I have always thought it odd that we moved away from the original intent of the Constitution when dealing with the executive branch so soon after it was created. The choosing of the vice president from those at odds with him or her for the position seems to me to have been the way to go. Knowing that the "other guy" might take your job if you are removed and most probably take the country in a completely different direction is a formidable threat and motivator to keep your nose clean and do your level best in office.

What follows was superseded by the 12th Amendment:

Each State shall appoint, in such Manner as the Legislature thereof may direct, a Number of Electors, equal to the whole Number of Senators and Representatives to which the State may be entitled in the Congress: but no Senator or Representative, or Person holding an Office of Trust or Profit under the United States, shall be appointed an Elector. The Electors shall meet in their respective States, and vote by Ballot for two Persons, of whom one at least shall not be an Inhabitant of the same State with themselves. And they shall make a List of all the Persons voted for, and of the Number of Votes for each; which List they shall sign and certify, and transmit sealed to the Seat of the Government of the United States, directed to the President of the Senate. The President of the Senate shall, in the Presence of the Senate and House of Representatives, open all the Certificates, and the Votes shall then be counted. The Person having the greatest Number of Votes shall be the President, if such Number be a Majority of the whole Number of Electors appointed; and if there be more than one who have such Majority, and have an equal Number of Votes, then the House of Representatives shall immediately chuse by Ballot one of them for President; and if no Person have a Majority, then from the five highest on the List the said House shall in like Manner chuse the President. But in chusing the President, the Votes shall be taken by States, the Representation from each State having one Vote; A quorum for this Purpose shall consist of a Member or Members from two thirds of the States, and a Majority of all the States shall be necessary to a Choice. In every Case, after the Choice of the President, the Person having the greatest Number of Votes of the Electors shall be the

Vice President. But if there should remain two or more who have equal Votes, the Senate shall chuse from them by Ballot the Vice President.

Although it was superseded by the 12th Amendment, we should still take a look at the preceding to better understand what was being protected against in its very being.

It appears that the original intend was that the people not be so completely involved in the choosing of the president. They were to be represented, again, by the states who would choose and charge electors to represent the people. I must conclude that this was the better plan inasmuch as the great mass of Americans at the time lacked the understanding of their own personal freedom and did not fully grasp the Constitution and the freedoms and responsibilities of citizenship that were found within it. Am I claiming that Americans at the time were too stupid to undertake such a selection? No. I am, however, suggesting that democracy in a republic is best represented when it is allowed to operate as such. We do not live in a democracy in the truest terms of the word.

Our nation was set up as a republic and as such we the people choose electors to represent our individual interests in the greater federalized system. In fact, in reading the 12th Amendment you will notice there was not much changed from this section in Article 2. Read the following and you will recognize that the choosing of the president still lies with this same body of electors. This is the Electoral College. Our popular vote is for all intents and purposes an exercise in mental masturbation. And, of course, today the vice president is not chosen by the people of the Electoral College but by the presidential candidates themselves. So much for democracy or a representative republic when it comes to the vice president.

12th Amendment:

The Electors shall meet in their respective states, and vote by ballot for President and Vice-President, one of whom, at least, shall not be an inhabitant of the same state with themselves; they shall name in their ballots the person voted for as President, and in distinct ballots the person voted for as Vice-President, and they shall make distinct lists of all persons voted for as President, and of all persons voted for as Vice-President and of the number of votes for each, which lists they shall sign and certify, and transmit sealed to the seat of the government of the United States, directed to the President of the Senate; The President of the Senate shall, in the presence of the Senate and House of Representatives, open all the certificates and the votes shall then be counted; The person having the greatest Number of votes for President, shall be the President, if such number be a majority of the whole number of Electors appointed; and if no person have such majority, then from the persons having the highest numbers not exceeding three on the list of those voted for as President, the House of Representatives shall choose immediately, by ballot, the President. But in choosing the President, the votes shall be taken by states, the representation from each state having one vote; a quorum for this purpose shall consist of a member or members from two-thirds of the states and a majority of all the states shall be necessary to a choice. And if the House of Representatives shall not choose a President whenever the right of choice shall devolve upon them, before the fourth day of March next following, then the Vice-President shall act as President, as in the case of the death or other constitutional disability of the President. The person having the greatest number of votes as Vice-President, shall be the Vice-President, if such number be a majority of the whole number of Electors appointed, and if no person have a majority, then from the two highest numbers on the list, the Senate shall choose the Vice-President; a quorum for the purpose shall consist of two-thirds of the whole number of Senators, and a majority of the whole number shall be necessary to a choice.

But no person constitutionally ineligible to the office of President shall be eligible to that of Vice-President of the United States.

"The Congress may determine the Time of chusing the Electors, and the Day on which they shall give their Votes; which Day shall be the same throughout the United States."

This simply reads that Congress picks the date for elections for the presidency. It also mandates that they remain consistent throughout the country.

"No Person except a natural born Citizen, or a Citizen of the United States, at the time of the Adoption of this Constitution, shall be eligible to the Office of President; neither shall any Person be eligible to that Office who shall not have attained to the Age of thirty five Years, and been fourteen Years a Resident within the United States."

The specifics of this are clear. The person seeking the presidency will be a natural-born citizen. What does this mean exactly? It means they will be born within the United States or in one of the many areas constituting the United States. An example of having not been born in one of the fifty states yet still being a natural-born American is represented in Senator John McCain. John McCain was born in the Panamanian Zone when the United States still controlled the Panama Canal. Those areas held and operated by the US are as much a part of the United States as any military base on the face of the earth.

Continuing, obviously there were people who were not born in the US prior to the passage of the Constitution as they would have been born under the crown of Great Britain or could possibly have been from any number of other countries, which is why the statement "or a Citizen of the United States, at the time of the Adoption of this Constitution" was added. This allowed those who were every bit as committed to the new nation to lead it without having been born on US soil at the time. However, it is interesting to note that not one of those early presidents or any since have ever been born anywhere other than on US soil. (Present executive eligibility questions have not yet been answered and as such I will refrain from pronouncing him eligible to serve.)

The president must be thirty-five years of age and have been in country for more than fourteen years. The age of thirty-five was considered by most as a reasonable age when your world knowledge and experience would suit you to the task. The fourteen-year provision is most likely to ensure those entering the race were truly committed to the nation and fourteen years of living here would suggest that. However, today it does not matter as much because you could live overseas for many years then return and decide to run for office.

> In Case of the Removal of the President from Office, or of his Death, Resignation, or Inability to discharge the Powers and Duties of the said Office, the Same shall devolve on the Vice President, and the Congress may by Law provide for the Case of Removal, Death, Resignation or Inability, both of the President and Vice President, declaring what Officer shall then act as President, and such Officer shall act accordingly, until the Disability be removed, or a President shall be elected.

This was later clarified in the 20th and 25th Amendments—Presidential Disability and Succession. The declaration of the new president of who would move to what chair in the shuffle upon the death or removal of the former president left too much to chance in a representative republic. Seems that mattered again in 1967....

"The President shall, at stated Times, receive for his Services, a Compensation, which shall neither be encreased nor diminished during the Period for which he shall have been elected, and he shall not receive within that Period any other Emolument from the United States, or any of them."

Yes, people, we actual pay for this representation. Can you believe it? And a pretty penny I might add. It comes to $400,000 a year, a free one-hundred-plus-room mansion, a chef, multiple cars, a pair of planes, and all the security you could ask for. The only bummer is that if you sign in to affect a pay raise, it can't start during your term. You give the raise to the next president.

"Before he enter on the Execution of his Office, he shall take the following Oath or Affirmation: 'I do solemnly swear (or affirm) that I will faithfully execute the Office of President of the United States, and will to the best of my Ability, preserve, protect and defend the Constitution of the United States.'"

This is the Oath of Office that all presidents must take. It is simple, eloquent, and reasonable. However, several presidents in the past (and I might add currently) seem to lose track of what the Constitution actually says.

"Section. 2. The President shall be Commander in Chief of the Army and Navy of the United States, and of the Militia of the several States, when called into the actual Service of the United States; he may require the Opinion, in writing, of the principal Officer in each of the executive Departments, upon any Subject relating to the Duties of their respective Offices, and he shall have Power to grant Reprieves and Pardons for Offences against the United States, except in Cases of Impeachment."

Commander in chief clause. The president runs the show in our military as a civilian representative of the people. He may use any one of his officers at his disposal for advice in regards to that or any sworn duty he has. This does not mean Czars. It means Senate-confirmed officers of the executive branch. In addition, he can pardon all crimes save impeachment.

"He shall have Power, by and with the Advice and Consent of the Senate, to make Treaties, provided two thirds of the Senators present concur; and he shall nominate, and by and with the Advice and Consent of the Senate, shall appoint Ambassadors, other public Ministers and Consuls, Judges of the supreme Court, and all other Officers of the United States, whose Appointments are not herein otherwise provided for, and which shall be established by Law: but the Congress may by Law vest the Appointment of such inferior Officers, as they think proper, in the President alone, in the Courts of Law, or in the Heads of Departments."

The president can negotiate any treaty he wants, but it means nothing unless a two-third majority of the Senate approves it. He can pick the Supreme Court, ambassadors, and his cabinet with the consent of Congress. Checks and balances from the start. Czars, however, never go through this vetting process so if you are wondering why many of us get upset about it, that's why.

"The President shall have Power to fill up all Vacancies that may happen during the Recess of the Senate, by granting Commissions which shall expire at the End of their next Session."

These are temporary appointments that you don't hear about much any more, mostly because of the issue of placing a person in a position when you know they will not get confirmed just means you have to start the process over again, so you might as well do it right from the start.

"Section. 3. He shall from time to time give to the Congress Information of the State of the Union, and recommend to their Consideration such Measures as he shall judge necessary and expedient; he may, on extraordinary Occasions, convene both Houses, or either of them, and in Case of Disagreement between them, with Respect to the Time of Adjournment, he may adjourn them to such Time as he shall think proper; he shall receive Ambassadors and other public Ministers; he shall take Care that the Laws be faithfully executed, and shall Commission all the Officers of the United States."

The State of the Union has not always been given live in Congress. It has been sent via letter in the past if you can believe that. In today's society I cannot imagine a politician missing any opportunity to stand in front of the cameras. But the president must give the Congress an update from "time to time." Today we expect that this is done yearly.

The president's power to adjourn Congress is not really an issue as Congress has a pretty set schedule these days. Its leadership pretty much handles this, keeping the president out of the mix.

The receiving of world leaders is solely the president's job. He meets, chats, negotiates, and befriends many on behalf of the people. Great gig if you can get it.

He also appoints the officers in the military. This is one of the highest honors a president can perform; however, it is nearly always done without his presence.

"Section. 4. The President, Vice President and all civil Officers of the United States, shall be removed from Office on Impeachment for, and Conviction of, Treason, Bribery, or other high Crimes and Misdemeanors."

"High Crimes and Misdemeanors," if only someone would have been a bit more specific. Treason and bribery, those are easy to understand, but at what point is a misdemeanor defined and what about a high crime? The jury is still out on this and will be for eternity. Jefferson was accused of such, as was Clinton. Clinton certainly lied under oath about Monica Lewinsky and Nixon, while not having broken into the Watergate himself, certainly did not help his case by running the cover-up to hide it after the fact.

One thing that one must come away with from Article 2 is that the power of the presidency was and is extremely limited. And while it is not the shortest article in the Constitution for what is certainly perceived as the most powerful man in America, it seems far too short for its importance.

# Article 3—Sections 1, 2, and 3

Before we get going on this section I need to once again stress the use of the word shall and define it as the framers used it. Shall means will, and shall not means will not. Some have claimed that "shall" meant or was used as "should or might" but, clearly, and you will see it here in this article as nowhere else in the Constitution, "shall" means "will," leaving no room for interpretation. In order to find the roots for their usage of it you need look no further than the Bible. Thou shall not ... thou shall ... were not in any way open to interpretation and the founders, while not all Christian, were certainly familiar with the Biblical text and the usage and force that the word shall brought to bear on any subject matter.

"Section. 1. The judicial Power of the United States, shall be vested in one supreme Court, and in such inferior Courts as the Congress may from time to time ordain and establish. The Judges, both of the supreme and inferior Courts, shall hold their Offices during good Behaviour, and shall, at stated Times, receive for their Services, a Compensation, which shall not be diminished during their Continuance in Office."

In this opening section of Article 3 we clearly see that the Supreme Court and the inferior courts are to be fully vested with all the judicial power. It makes arrangements for the lifetime appointment of Supreme Court justices, stating they "shall hold their Offices during good Behaviour" and not for a set number of years. This was done in order to remove the justices from the political process so that their full focus could be on the Constitution and the law, freeing them from political pressures to rule in any particular way other than the legally prescribed method spelled out in the Constitution.

Had lifetime appointment not been secured or a submissive relationship to either the Congress or the president not been secured against, undue influence would have been placed on the Court to rule in accordance with the wishes of one or the other branches of government. Upon the appointment of a seat on the high court, the president has already secured to some extent preferential treatment of the Constitution to his or her interpretation but he or she has done so with the consent of Congress, thereby eliminating any suggestion of tampering with the courts. (If only this was the end of the matter but we all know better than that.)

"Section. 2. The judicial Power shall extend to all Cases, in Law and Equity, arising under this Constitution, the Laws of the United States, and Treaties made, or which shall be made, under their Authority;—to all Cases affecting Ambassadors, other public Ministers and Consuls;—to all Cases of admiralty and maritime Jurisdiction;—to Controversies to which the United States shall be a Party;—to Controversies between two or more States;—between a State and Citizens of another State;—

between Citizens of different States;—between Citizens of the same State claiming Lands under Grants of different States, and between a State, or the Citizens thereof, and foreign States, Citizens or Subjects."

This section clarifies over whom Supreme Court decisions will be binding.

From 1789 to 1803 the US Supreme Court was a minor player in the US Government but in 1803, in Marbury v. Madison, the Court for the first time ever struck down an act of Congress on the grounds that it was unconstitutional. In doing so Chief Justice John Marshall gave rise to enormous power in the Supreme Court. In claiming to be the guardians of the Constitution the Court held that "any law in conflict with the Constitution cannot be enforced in the courts" (American Political Dictionary, 8th edition. Plano/Greenberg: Saunders College Publishing, 1989). With this in mind portions of the act were simply tossed out. While not mentioned in the Constitution, this is where the idea of judicial review originates; today it is considered a normal part of the Supreme Court's duties. Only problem is, it isn't. The act should have been returned to Congress to have them "fix" the issues. In striking down any portion of any law the Supreme Court is legislating, altering the act or law. This creation of law is the sole providence of the Congress. It is the very reason the line item veto has never been granted to the president. It cannot pass Constitutional muster.

Later use of this review process has not only diminished some other laws by removing (again, altering the act or law) sections of law from the books, but it has also added or created from whole cloth rights not previously acknowledged that as such could not have been supported by precedence. Roe v. Wade is one such decision as was Dred Scott v. Sanford. One created a right to abortion on demand while the other reduced freedom to being based on one's skin color. One helped lead to the Civil War while the other has led to the deaths of over forty-three million Americans.

The point of all this is simply to point out that Supreme Court decisions are not without imperfection.

"In all Cases affecting Ambassadors, other public Ministers and Consuls, and those in which a State shall be Party, the supreme Court shall have original Jurisdiction. In all the other Cases before mentioned, the supreme Court shall have appellate Jurisdiction, both as to Law and Fact, with such Exceptions, and under such Regulations as the Congress shall make."

This means that only in those areas mentioned earlier is the Supreme Court the only court with jurisdiction to offer a ruling. In all other lower court decisions the Supreme Court is the final word should questions continue to arise on lower court rulings. Appeals courts for the federal court system were only established in the 1980s. Prior to that all federal court decisions could be brought directly to the Supreme Court. When Congress virtually eliminated the mandatory review process with the creation of the federal appellant court system they also gave the Supreme Court the ability to create their own docket. Now if the Supreme Court does not take on an appeal the lower court ruling becomes the ultimate decision.

"The Trial of all Crimes, except in Cases of Impeachment, shall be by Jury; and such Trial shall be held in the State where the said Crimes shall have been committed; but when not committed within any State, the Trial shall be at such Place or Places as the Congress may by Law have directed."

The Supreme Court does not try cases of crime. They only deal with questions of the constitutionality of decisions handed down in trials of crimes or other acts in which the constitutionality of a decision may be in question. Only in the case of impeachment is the Supreme Court the direct court of trial. All other cases are to be handled by the court system in the state in which the crime was committed. And if the crime was not committed in a state (leaving territories, ships, and possible air travel) it is to be taken up in a place prescribed by Congress.

"Section. 3. Treason against the United States, shall consist only in levying War against them, or in adhering to their Enemies, giving them Aid and Comfort. No Person shall be convicted of Treason unless on the Testimony of two Witnesses to the same overt Act, or on Confession in open Court."

Treason has been levied against only fifteen people in US history that I could find. Many were pardoned, some executed, and others served time. Treason has been levied against common folks and presidents (FDR and Truman by McCarthy) although most accused of treason in the press have never been formally charged. Although the case could be made that many who today serve in government have committed treasonous acts, proving it to constitutional definitions would be hard due mainly to our skewed system of justice following decades of precedent.

"The Congress shall have Power to declare the Punishment of Treason, but no Attainder of Treason shall work Corruption of Blood, or Forfeiture except during the Life of the Person attainted."

In plain English, the descendants of someone convicted of treason cannot be held responsible or be punished as they were in Great Britain at the time. I also found that while property can be confiscated it must be inheritable at the time of the guilty one's death.

It is interesting how much the Supreme Court has changed over the years and mostly by their own hand. Today's Supreme Court strikes down law, creates law, and finds hidden meanings to words that are not in the Constitution. The idea that an originalist court would be good for America is one whose time has come. Reducing the Court back to its constitutionally prescribed intention would be the best thing this country could do for itself in the long run. However, with the stepping down of Justice Stevens in the near future and the radical leadership we currently have, chances are that a conservative court with members understanding the original intent of the constitution may be a long time off.

# Article 4—Sections 1, 2, 3, and 4

"Section. 1. Full Faith and Credit shall be given in each State to the public Acts, Records, and judicial Proceedings of every other State. And the Congress may by general Laws prescribe the Manner in which such Acts, Records and Proceedings shall be proved, and the Effect thereof."

This section deals with the simple issue of legal acts enforced in one state shall be upheld in the others. This is why the issue of gay marriage is so contentious. Should a couple be married in Maine then they are considered married in New York without having to go through a New York ceremony. If one is considered a felon in California they are a felon in Hawaii. In the case of marriage Congress "prescribed" the marriage license. It "proved" to any other state that the act of marriage was done in accordance with that state's law. With some states legalizing gay marriage and others not, it is going to create at some point a constitutional question that only the Supreme Court can decide. At contention is the rights of spouses, regardless of sex, to inherit property, made medical decisions, decide the fate of minor children, etc.

"Section. 2. Clause 1: The Citizens of each State shall be entitled to all Privileges and Immunities of Citizens in the several States."

Stated plainly, as if it is needed, you are free and equal in all the states, not just the one of your birth or current citizenship.

"Clause 2: A Person charged in any State with Treason, Felony, or other Crime, who shall flee from Justice, and be found in another State, shall on Demand of the executive Authority of the State from which he fled, be delivered up, to be removed to the State having Jurisdiction of the Crime."

Extradition between the states is mandatory and no state can refuse to deliver an accused back to the state requesting it.

"Clause 3: No Person held to Service or Labour in one State, under the Laws thereof, escaping into another, shall, in Consequence of any Law or Regulation therein, be discharged from such Service or Labour, but shall be delivered up on Claim of the Party to whom such Service or Labour may be due."

The 13th Amendment ended this practice as it pertained to slavery, which was made illegal by that amendment.

"Section. 3. Clause 1: New States may be admitted by the Congress into this Union; but no new State shall be formed or erected within the Jurisdiction of any other State; nor any State be formed by the Junction of two or more States, or Parts of States, without the Consent of the Legislatures of the States concerned as well as of the Congress."

Pretty straightforward, the clause instructs us on how new states are to be formed, and, more importantly, how they are not to be formed. Many people think the issue of adding states today is pretty much a historical one; however, Puerto Rico has a state request that comes up periodically, and Californians have toyed repeatedly over the last forty years with splitting the state into two or even three separate states. California is in a unique situation, having a population larger than that of Canada with a majority in the south. Those in the north and central parts of the state feel their impact is negated by sheer numbers. It would be an interesting situation should it ever come to pass considering the staggering debt carried in the state and the division of land in question.

"Clause 2: The Congress shall have Power to dispose of and make all needful Rules and Regulations respecting the Territory or other Property belonging to the United States; and nothing in this Constitution shall be so construed as to Prejudice any Claims of the United States, or of any particular State."

This is the clause that grants Congress the right to run Washington DC. It enabled Congress to manage the territories prior to statehood and many other smaller claims our country has on a number of places including the US Virgin Isles, American Samoa (prior to 1962; today it is administered by the Department of the Interior through local elections), and Navassa Island.

"Section. 4. The United States shall guarantee to every State in this Union a Republican Form of Government, and shall protect each of them against Invasion; and on Application of the Legislature, or of the Executive (when the Legislature cannot be convened) against domestic Violence."

In all the Constitution this is the one place you can clearly se what the federal government's true role is: protecting the states. Defense is the only clearly enumerated role of the federal government although, as we discussed earlier, the general welfare clause (which isn't a clause at all) has been stretched to cover just about every aspect of American life from cradle to grave.

# Article 5

The Congress, whenever two thirds of both Houses shall deem it necessary, shall propose Amendments to this Constitution, or, on the Application of the Legislatures of two thirds of the several States, shall call a Convention for proposing Amendments, which, in either Case, shall be valid to all Intents and Purposes, as Part of this Constitution, when ratified by the Legislatures of three fourths of the several States, or by Conventions in three fourths thereof, as the one or the other Mode of Ratification may be proposed by the Congress; Provided that no Amendment which may be made prior to the Year One thousand eight hundred and eight shall in any Manner affect the first and fourth Clauses in the Ninth Section of the first Article; and that no State, without its Consent, shall be deprived of its equal Suffrage in the Senate.

Here we find the what's, who's, and how's of amending the US Constitution. But we also see another possibly more intriguing mention; that of the Constitutional Convention called for by the states themselves: "or, on the Application of the Legislatures of two thirds of the several States, shall call a Convention for proposing Amendments, which, in either Case, shall be valid to all Intents and Purposes, as Part of this Constitution, when ratified by the Legislatures of three fourths of the several States." One thing that must be understood on this point; should two-thirds of the states ever call for a Constitutional Convention the entire Constitution would be open for debate, not just a simple amendment to it. This is dangerous, but it also is another safeguard against a federal government gone mad. The states hold the ultimate power to reconfigure this government constitutionally. Please understand that point.

The other point that needs mention here is a portion of that closing line: "and that no State, without its Consent, shall be deprived of its equal Suffrage in the Senate." Suffrage is defined as "The right or privilege of voting; franchise" and "The exercise of such a right." Way back in the beginning of this section of the book we touched on the Senate election process found in Article 1, Section 3, and the modifications made by the 17th Amendment that changed the way senators were elected. Think for moment about your representation in any government body, whether in an HOA or even a board of directors for a company. Those electing people to those positions are the people to whom those positions will be most apt to represent. Today the states effectively have no representation in Washington because of the 17th Amendment. Yet the states hold the power to call the whole thing off. It can be a touchy situation in the future.

# Article 6

"Clause 1: All Debts contracted and Engagements entered into, before the Adoption of this Constitution, shall be as valid against the United States under this Constitution, as under the Confederation."

Here we find the congruence of debt from the old Confederation of States to the new and improved, or, as the founders said, "more perfect Union."

"Clause 2: This Constitution, and the Laws of the United States which shall be made in Pursuance thereof; and all Treaties made, or which shall be made, under the Authority of the United States, shall be the supreme Law of the Land; and the Judges in every State shall be bound thereby, any Thing in the Constitution or Laws of any State to the Contrary notwithstanding."

"The Supreme Law of the Land," so long as it was ratified and approved. Yet at the end of the day the Constitution itself is the supreme law of the land as nothing passed by Congress or the executive can stand in contrast to the Constitution.

"Clause 3: The Senators and Representatives before mentioned, and the Members of the several State Legislatures, and all executive and judicial Officers, both of the United States and of the several States, shall be bound by Oath or Affirmation, to support this Constitution; but no religious Test shall ever be required as a Qualification to any Office or public Trust under the United States."

In my disgust with the way thing operate today I truly wish this were the case. Although an oath is administered to all elected officials we have only too often been reminded that humans are fallible and those we elect are most often no better than any other.

And although no religious test is to be administered, every leader we have ever had has been tested at some point on his or her religious views. Just look at the last healthcare reform bill to be passed. It was on religious grounds that Mr. Stupak said he would not vote for the bill ... just prior to actually voting for the bill anyway. (Don't know who Stupak is, Google it. I'm not doing all the work for you.)

# Article 7

"The Ratification of the Conventions of nine States, shall be sufficient for the Establishment of this Constitution between the States so ratifying the Same."

"Done in Convention by the Unanimous Consent of the States present the Seventeenth Day of September in the Year of our Lord one thousand seven hundred and Eighty seven and of the Independence of the United States of America the Twelfth In witness whereof We have hereunto subscribed our Names."

And with that final declaration, the founders signed their names, but even that was not all done on the same day....

# Closing Remarks

The Constitution is the cornerstone on which our country was founded. And although it can be changed we do so often at our peril. The unintended circumstances that arise are often far worse than the problem we think we are solving.

Its changes have both hurt and benefitted the country and its people. From allowing abortion to ending slavery, it has been done for the most ethical of reasons and the most hideous of reasons.

Moving forward Americans need to do two things above all others:
1. Know our history, our roots, and the reason we created this government.
2. Understand that the future is as bright as we want it to be and that only by moving forward with ideas based on these age-old ideals will we ever succeed to the pinnacle of the promise given to us by our Founding Fathers.

www.ingramcontent.com/pod-product-compliance
Lightning Source LLC
Chambersburg PA
CBHW030434290526

45786CB00001B/285